Henry Cecil was the ｜ Leon. He was born in Norwood Green Rectory, near London, England in 1902. He studied at Cambridge where he edited an undergraduate magazine and wrote a Footlights May Week production. Called to the bar in 1923, he served with the British Army during the Second World War. While in the Middle East with his battalion he used to entertain the troops with a serial story each evening. This formed the basis of his first book, *Full Circle*. He was appointed a County Court Judge in 1949 and held that position until 1967. The law and the circumstances which surround it were the source of his many novels, plays, and short stories. His books are works of great comic genius with unpredictable twists of plot which highlight the often absurd workings of the English legal system. He died in 1976.

FULL CIRCLE

by

Henry Cecil

HOUSE OF STRATUS

First published in 1948

Copyright by Henry Cecil

All rights reserved. No part of this publication may be reproduced, stored in a
retrieval system, or transmitted, in any form, or by any means (electronic,
mechanical, photocopying, recording, or otherwise), without the prior permission
of the publisher. Any person who does any unauthorised act in relation to this
publication may be liable to criminal prosecution and civil claims for damages.

The right of Henry Cecil to be identified as the author of this work has been
asserted.

This edition published in 2000 by House of Stratus, an imprint of
Stratus Books Ltd., 21 Beeching Park, Kelly Bray,
Cornwall, PL17 8QS, UK.

www.houseofstratus.com

Typeset, printed and bound by House of Stratus.

A catalogue record for this book is available from the British Library
and the Library of Congress.

ISBN 1-84232-054-8

This book is sold subject to the condition that it shall not be lent, resold, hired
out, or otherwise circulated without the publisher's express prior consent in any
form of binding, or cover, other than the original as herein published and without
a similar condition being imposed on any subsequent purchaser, or bona fide
possessor.

This is a fictional work and all characters are drawn from the author's imagination.
Any resemblances or similarities to persons either living or dead
are entirely coincidental.

Contents

CHAPTER ONE

The Confession

As the train drew into Cambridge Station, Professor Melton stepped on to the platform. He had just arrived from Harvard University, where, for many years, he had been teaching Roman law and jurisprudence. He was an Englishman, but, after a brilliant academic career and a few years' practice at the Bar, he had migrated to Harvard. Recently, however, he had felt an urge to return to his own country, and, being offered the Chair of Jurisprudence at Cambridge, he immediately accepted. He had acquired a very big reputation, and his books on jurisprudence and Roman law had become standard works both in America and England.

Most of his pupils found his lectures somewhat heavy and completely lacking in any humour to leaven them. By his fellow professors, however, he was considered the leading authority on both subjects and his views were looked upon almost as a judgment of the House of Lords. He had been an undergraduate at St James' and it was to St James' that he was returning. He was delighted at the prospect, and during the journey he had been revelling in the thought of renewing old friendships and of seeing again the place where he had spent such a happy four years of his life.

No doubt his eagerness to arrive as soon as possible was the cause of his stepping on to the platform before the train had come to a standstill. He was thrown quite heavily to the ground and his head struck something hard. He was dazed for the moment but not rendered unconscious. Porters soon arrived to give assistance and he was lifted up and taken into the waiting-room. There, to his relief, he found that he had merely bruised his body and bumped his head. There were no bones broken and the bump on his head, though unpleasant, was nothing more than a bump. His luggage was collected for him, and in due course he arrived in a taxi at St James'. He was soon with the Master, who had been an undergraduate with him, and, apart from referring casually to his little accident, he soon forgot all about it. His joy at regaining touch with Cambridge and all that it had meant to him was even greater than he had expected, and it gave him a considerable thrill to visit his old rooms. He dined in Hall, and sat up till late in the Common Room discussing the years which had passed.

Although he had the Chair of Jurisprudence he had arranged to lecture on Roman law as well. The term was one day old when he arrived and his first lecture was to take place two days later. He was to deliver a series of lectures on "The Principles of Jurisprudence" which were intended, in the main, for students who had only begun to study the subject. The series was one of sixteen lectures, two each week in an eight-week term. He was giving a similar series on Roman law, and, in addition, he had small classes of pupils in both subjects. He was likely, therefore, to be kept busy, and he was pleased at the thought, for his great interest in life was his work.

Punctually at the advertised time he arrived at the lecture room to deliver his first lecture. As he stood up to begin, he felt a most curious sensation in his head and was surprised to find himself opening his lecture in these terms: "Ladies and gentlemen, I'm sure you would all prefer to be outside – on the river or playing tennis or the like – rather than listening to a lecture on jurisprudence. It is a dry subject and I believe I am considered an unusually boring lecturer. I said 'ladies and gentlemen,' but you will forgive me if I really think of you as boys and girls. There is such youth and charm about all of you. I should hate to think that, as you leave this lecture room, you should do so with less sparkle in your eyes and minds because of anything which I had done or said. Nevertheless, I have to address you for the appointed time. Perhaps there is a way out of the difficulty. Perhaps I can find something to say which might amuse you. Are you in the least bit interested in the juridical conceptions of right and wrong? Obviously not. Nor, at any rate at the moment, am I. Put away your pens and pencils, then, shut up your notebooks, and I will try to entertain you for the hour allotted to me. Here is a story which certainly has a good deal to do with wrong, if it has little to do with right. It is called 'The Confession.' I hope you will like it."

The Confession

I am writing in prison. I wish the light were a little better, as I want to finish this tonight. I have something very important to do in the morning.

This time I am going to tell the whole truth, and it is a little difficult to know where to begin. Perhaps that Friday afternoon, when I was walking away from the Old Bailey during the luncheon adjournment, will be a good jumping-off ground. I had been watching a murder trial. Charles Cordwell was the man charged. He was indicted for the

3

murder of his son – a most unpleasant affair, but not more unpleasant than the son himself. I knew the family well. Charles was a widower with a son George and a daughter Anne. George was a complete scoundrel, and his father was continually being compelled to pay very large sums to keep him out of gaol. It would have been very much better if he hadn't paid them, but he always did. George invariably promised that it would be the last time, and, of course, it never was. Anne was – well, I had been in love with her for some time and my description might be prejudiced. So, as it is to be the truth this time, I won't take any chances. You must imagine her for yourself.

It was she who interrupted my thoughts on that Friday afternoon. "How is it going?" she said anxiously. I hesitated. "Tell me the truth."

"As badly as it could."

There was no point in lying. I'll tell you the case against Charles. He had been a wealthy man, but George's escapades had caused him to dip heavily into capital and eventually to mortgage his house. It was a large house in the country – the sort of place where all kinds of people met. It was not a long way from the station and it was usually possible for friends of the family to walk into it at any time. Shortly before the murder Charles had had to pay something like £15,000 to cover up George's last swindle. As a result, his only asset was a policy on George's life. Charles had always believed in life insurance as an investment, and, as soon as George was old enough, he had insured his life for a very large sum. It was a sum big enough to retrieve Charles' dwindling fortune – particularly as it couldn't be obtained until George was out of the way. Well, one morning, George was found by the gardener in a summerhouse in the Cordwells' garden with a bullet in his brain and a revolver close beside him. The gardener went at once to find Charles, but Charles wasn't to be found. The police were called and, on examination, the revolver was found to have Charles' fingerprints on it. He had left the house suddenly without telling anyone, and no one could think of any innocent reason for his hurried departure. It seemed a clear case. The police went after Charles. He evaded them for a day or two, but was eventually arrested. At first he denied any knowledge of George's death and said he was called away on urgent business the night before the murder. He couldn't, however, give any very clear account of what the business was; he couldn't account for his fingerprints being on the revolver, and eventually he admitted that his story was untrue. He then said that he had found George dead in the summerhouse with a revolver in his hand. He had examined the body to see if it was alive and taken the revolver out of his hand. He was about to go for the police when he suddenly became terrified. He realised that he had been heard quarrelling with George the previous day. The revolver was his, and, worst of all, he was the person who would most benefit from George's death. He thought he would be suspected, tried and hanged. He lost his nerve and ran away. That was also the reason why he lied at first to the police. Not a very convincing story. Doctors were called to give evidence both by the prosecution and the defence. The doctor called by the prosecution said that the wound could not have been self-inflicted. The doctor called for the defence said that it could have been, although it would not have been too easy.

"I suppose you mean," said prosecuting counsel, "that, if the dead man had been a Japanese contortionist, he might have managed it."

"Well, not quite as difficult as that," said the witness lamely.

That was the state of the case when the court adjourned for lunch. You can see now why I said it was going so badly. Anne looked at me. "You must do something," she said.

"What can I do? I am not a barrister any longer and, even if I were, I couldn't take over the case in the middle. Anyway, Olliphant is doing everything possible."

"You can do something, and you must," said Anne. "You know quite well what I mean. You're the only person who can help, and, if you do, I'll marry you; and, if you don't, I'll never speak to you again."

I thought for a moment. "All right," I said, "I'll do what I can, but you mustn't complain afterwards about my methods."

"I'll complain of nothing if you will only get him off. I know he can't have murdered George. He could never have done it."

"It looks very black," I said.

"Well, perform one of your conjuring tricks and make it white, then," she said, and left me.

I'm afraid this conversation must have puzzled you. Why should Anne think I could help? The evidence against her father was almost conclusive; he was caught in the machinery of the criminal law and he was being quite fairly tried. What could anyone do? Well, I'll explain. I was called to the Bar when I was twenty-one, and, after the first few years of waiting, I started to acquire an extensive practice. Then, all of a sudden, as the result of an unfortunate episode, I was not only disbarred but sent to prison. It was entirely my own fault. I had been doing a case one hot summer day before Mr Justice Plank. He was even more dense than usual. He tried the case hopelessly and was extremely rude to me. Finally, he gave judgment against my client – quite wrongly, as my opponent would have been the first to admit – and in his decision he said, in effect, that my conduct of the case had prejudiced my client's chances of success. I was very angry and lost my temper. I forget exactly what I said, but I did mention something about "a blithering old idiot." Plank nearly had an apoplectic fit and demanded an apology. I said, "What for?" and left the court. I was reported to the Benchers of my Inn and disbarred. I thought it rather hard to be ruined for one piece of bad temper, and it made me see red. I went to Plank's court. Just before a case was about to start I got up and said, "I hope you're happy now."

"Take him away," said Plank, and sent me to prison for six weeks for contempt of court.

I spent them in Brixton, which is reserved mostly for prisoners on remand and people in contempt of court. After I'd been there a day or two I began to take stock of my position. What was I to do when I came out? Practice of the law was barred to me and I had no other accomplishments. Strangely enough, I was not dispirited. I was even rather excited at the idea of striking out afresh, though I could not think in what direction. I talked to my co-prisoners and found some of them extremely interesting. One little burglar, whose confidence I won, described his methods to me. They were highly ingenious. Then I learned quite a lot from a most amusing confidence trickster. From these small beginnings I suddenly thought of a means of livelihood in which I could employ my knowledge of the law. It was, I am afraid, thoroughly antisocial, but I had given up caring about that. I had noticed how these expert criminals were continually being caught and convicted in spite of their knowledge and experience. It soon became clear to me that, had they made proper plans for a possible capture, had they thought of the right story to tell, had they arranged a good alibi in advance, many of them would never even have been tried, while those that were tried would have had a very good chance of an acquittal.

So, when I came out, I started my underground bureau for making crime pay. I had a few introductions from my recent acquaintances in Brixton, and gradually my reputation in the underworld spread. I was a huge success. Criminals came from all parts of the country, and even from abroad, to consult me, and I must have been accessory to thousands of crimes which were never brought home to their perpetrators. I won't say that police court magistrates were driven out of business, but they certainly had more time to devote to their own wives and families – which shows that few actions are wholly bad in their results.

During my infamous career I met George Cordwell. In fact, I assisted him in one of his enterprises for which his father did *not* have to pay up. Through him I met Anne. Unfortunately for me, I fell in love with her, and, despite all my instincts of self-preservation, I eventually told her the truth about myself. Up till then I think I had been well in the running with her, but, after that confession, she would have nothing to do with me until that Friday afternoon when she sought my help. Now you see why she sought it.

But it is one thing to prepare an alibi for a crime in advance, and quite another to start to get someone off in the middle of his trial. However, the prize was a good one and I was determined to do my best. I had very little time. The evidence was concluded on the Friday and only speeches and summing up were left for the Monday. What could I do before those speeches to alter the whole aspect of the case? Faked evidence to suggest suicide occurred to me, but I ruled it out in view of what the doctors had said. That left only one other line of approach. If George had not killed himself someone had killed him. I must find a method of throwing suspicion on someone else. It would not be necessary to make out a cast-iron case against another man, but, if the jury could be shown that another man might have had a reason for killing him, and if I could manufacture some kind of evidence linking up that other man with the crime, it might be enough to throw a doubt on the guilt of the man in the dock.

I considered various people who had been let down by George, and the name of John Bostock at once occurred to me. Bostock was what I might call an all-rounder in the field of crime. He was a housebreaker, forger, bogus company promoter, and had various other criminal accomplishments. This is rare. Your real criminal is usually a specialist. He steals watches or bicycles, but seldom both. A long firm fraud had brought Bostock into association with George, and the latter had certainly got away with more than his fair share of the swag. Moreover, Bostock had actually been tried for his share in the swindle, and although, thanks to the efficiency of my service, he had been acquitted, he had always thought his arrest was due to a piece of double crossing by George. He was probably right. Having regard to Bostock's innumerable activities, I knew there were probably few occasions on which he would like to say truthfully where he had been. So I hit on the following plan. It was makeshift, but this was inevitable in view of the time factor.

I went to a police sergeant whom I knew to be out for promotion. I said to him, "I believe I can put you on to the man who really murdered George Cordwell."

He said, "He's in the dock."

I said, "That's what you think. Look here – it won't do you any harm – come along with me and see for yourself. If I'm wrong, no one will be any the worse off. If I'm right, there's a feather in your cap and an innocent man saved."

In the end he agreed. My idea was simply to walk in on John Bostock with the police sergeant, recite the grounds for his animosity against George together with some threats against George I'd heard (or would say I'd heard) him make, and then suddenly say to him, "You know you murdered George Cordwell. If you didn't, say where you were on the night of the murder, the 26th January." With any luck he would lie about his movements that day. By hunting around quickly I hoped to be able to prove he had lied when asked to account for his movements on the day of the murder. Not brilliant, I agree, but a possibility, and I had to do something.

Well, we couldn't find our man till Sunday night, but we ran him to ground then. I said my little piece and it went quite well until I came to the point where I asked him to account for his movements on the day of the murder. Then Bostock smiled.

"Well," he said, "it's a nasty confession to have to make, but, after all, it wasn't my fault, so why should I be ashamed? I regret to say that on the night in question and, indeed, for the previous two days I was in prison waiting trial on a most ridiculous charge of picking pockets in the Strand. I need hardly say that the magistrate dismissed the charge when he heard your – I mean my – explanation." It was all too true. The sergeant was very angry with me, and I was left only a few hours in which to produce something else to save Charles.

However, the power of love is strong and I refused to admit defeat. By the time the court sat on the Monday morning I had a completely new plan all ready and, what is more, I had told it to Charles' solicitor and to Olliphant, his counsel. They were amazed at what I said to them, but they were quite prepared to act on my statement.

Accordingly, when the court reassembled, Olliphant asked for permission to call another witness. The Judge gave him leave, and I stepped into the witness box and took the oath. Olliphant then said to the Judge that, in his view, the witness ought to be warned and would his Lordship be good enough to warn him. The Judge said that he presumed counsel knew what he was talking about, and, in a rather wearied tone (although it was only 10.30 in the morning), he told me that I was not bound to answer any questions which might incriminate me. Did I understand that? Yes, my Lord, I did.

"Very well – proceed, Mr Olliphant." Counsel then asked me to tell the court in my own words anything which I knew of my own knowledge relating to the guilt or innocence of the accused.

"I know he is innocent," I said.

"That is for the jury to decide," said the Judge. "If this witness has simply come to make a speech for the defence from the witness box under the guise of giving evidence, the sooner he leaves it the better."

Olliphant was unperturbed.

"My Lord, the witness said that he *knew* the accused was innocent, not that he thought or hoped or submitted that he was innocent." Then, turning to me, "Tell my Lord and the jury why you say you know the accused is innocent."

"Because I committed the murder myself and the accused had nothing to do with it."

There was a buzz of excitement in the court, followed by a sudden hush – rather like the hush which followed my calling Plank an old blitherer. The Judge was obviously shaken. He said nothing for a moment and then addressed me. "I have already warned you once, now I warn you again of two things – first that, if your statement on oath is true, you are liable to be tried for murder on your own confession; and secondly that, if it is not true, you are liable to be tried for perjury. I want you," he added, "to be particularly mindful of this second warning."

"My Lord," said Olliphant, "I don't know why your Lordship is hinting to the jury that the witness is committing perjury before he has given any details whatever of his statement."

"I do," said the Judge.

"May I ask why, then?" said Olliphant.

"You may not," said the Judge. "Continue with the evidence."

I then described to the court why and how I had committed the murder. The reasons I gave were my desire to be married to Anne; my objection to having a penniless father-in-law; the certainty that he would be penniless unless George were put out of the way. I then told how I shot George with his father's revolver. You must remember that I had been to the house often and that I was familiar with all the evidence in the case. I was able to describe exactly how and when I murdered George and how I had got away. My knowledge of the circumstances of the crime was such that my evidence could not be shaken in the least degree.

In cross-examination I was asked about the episode with Bostock and the police sergeant. Had I not tried to lay the blame on a completely innocent man, and was it not only when this failed that I decided to commit perjury to save the accused? It was quite true about Bostock, I said. Naturally I did not want to be hanged. That was why I never confessed until it seemed likely that the accused would be convicted. I had never thought for a moment that the accused would behave as stupidly as he did and so eventually compel me to take the course I was taking.

"Apparently," said counsel, "you did not mind Bostock hanging for a crime he had not committed."

"Well," I replied, "I can't say that his death would be of very much concern to me. He is not a great asset to the world. Nevertheless, there was no chance of his being convicted on his own trial; there would have been nothing like enough evidence to convict him; he would probably never have been sent for trial. Had my plan succeeded, I should have done no harm to him and, at the same time, I should have prevented an innocent man from being hanged."

Eventually, after more cross-examination and a little re-examination, my evidence was concluded, there was an adjournment for a few days and then the speeches began. Olliphant made an excellent little speech in which he defied the jury to convict Charles in the face of my evidence. Counsel for the prosecution said that it was no part of his duty to try to secure a conviction, and went on to tell the jury why they would be failing in their duty if they did not convict. Finally the Judge summed up, and I must say it was an extremely fair summing up. On the whole, it favoured the accused because he laid emphasis on the necessity for the absence of any reasonable doubt before the jury could convict. Had the evidence of a man who said he had committed the crime raised such a doubt? Defending counsel was quite justified in saying that the prosecution had not produced a single piece of evidence to show that my story was untrue. They had even been granted an adjournment to enable the police to check up on my movements, but nothing had resulted. The Judge had never had a case like it before, but that should not influence the jury in any way. The jury retired.

They returned in twenty minutes with a verdict of "Not Guilty."

The accused was discharged and I met an excited Anne in the corridor. "Well," I said, "that's all right," and then whispered, "Don't forget that your father can't be tried again, whatever further evidence may come to light; he has been acquitted and is safe for ever. Don't forget that."

"But, darling," she said, "what about you?"

"Oh, don't worry about me," I said. "I shall be quite all right," and at that moment an extremely polite detective inspector took me into custody on a charge of murdering George Cordwell.

I had been expecting this and was not in the least dismayed. In due course I appeared at a Metropolitan police court. Apart from a plan of the house and grounds, proof of the finding of the body, its condition, the fingerprints on the revolver, and similar matters, the only real evidence against me was my own sworn confession.

At the close of the case for the prosecution, the magistrate asked me what course I wished to take. Did I wish to give evidence or to call witnesses or what? I needn't do anything, but, if I did, it would all have to be taken down in writing. He didn't add that this would be a pity as he wanted to go out to tea with his wife. I'm afraid it wouldn't have altered my decision if he had. For one thing, that particular magistrate had annoyed me about a year previously by disbelieving one of my best stories – as told by a customer of mine – and sending him down for six months. Of course, he was acquitted on appeal to London Sessions, but I was annoyed at the extra trouble. Apart, however, from mere pettiness on my part it was important to call evidence at the police court.

This is a comparatively unusual proceeding in cases which are likely to be sent for trial. It gives the police an opportunity of disproving the story told by the defence and prevents the prisoner thinking up a better story before the actual hearing. However, my case was different.

"I wish to give evidence and call witnesses," I said.

"How many witnesses?" asked the magistrate.

"Four," I said.

"Four?" queried the magistrate's clerk sadly. He also had an appointment.

"Four," I said firmly.

"Very well then," said the magistrate. "Remanded for a week." So he kept his appointment after all.

Next week I went into the witness box. I admitted that I had confessed to the murder but I flatly denied that I had committed it. I only confessed so as to procure the acquittal of the father of the girl I wanted to marry. I was out of the house at the time of the murder. I was miles away. I was with several other people the whole time. They were at the court and would be called as witnesses. The police could spend any of their spare time checking up on this alibi between my committal and trial. That was why I had called evidence at the police court and, I added, spent an extra seven days in prison as a result. I was not cross-examined by the prosecution. They wanted to think about it and there was very little to ask me.

Then Messrs Hinks, Shorter, Snape and Drew gave evidence. They all were able to recall the relevant date. They all had particular and excellent reasons for being able to remember it. They all said they were with me. Either this was gross perjury or I could not have committed the murder. The magistrate sent me for trial.

I duly appeared at the Old Bailey before Mr Justice Pennant. Counsel for the prosecution was obviously not very happy about the case. It was plain from his opening that the police had been unable to do anything to my alibi.

"The case rests almost entirely on the prisoner's sworn confession," he said.

"Almost entirely?" said the Judge. "What else is there?"

"Well, my Lord, there is really hardly anything else."

"Mr Crump," said his Lordship, "you use words of qualification – *almost* entirely – *hardly* anything else. If you mean 'entirely' and 'nothing else,' please say so. If, on the other hand, there is anything besides the prisoner's confession, I shall want to know why it does not appear on the depositions."

"If your Lordship pleases," said Mr Crump, and turned again to continue his address to the jury.

"Yes, but what about it, Mr Crump?" continued the Judge. "You can't answer an awkward question by saying 'If your Lordship pleases.' Some counsel may do, but it is not satisfactory to me. Please do me the courtesy of answering my questions, however awkward they may be." Before counsel could reply the Judge turned to me and said, "There's nothing to smile about; you're on a very serious charge, and, anyway, you must behave yourself."

"If your Lordship pleases," I said.

The Judge blew his nose and then said, "Well, Mr Crump?"

"My Lord, the evidence, apart from merely formal evidence, rests entirely on the prisoner's confession."

"Thank you, Mr Crump," said his Lordship. "Now can't you see how much easier that makes it for the jury?" It certainly did. From start to finish the case was a walkover. I had to admit that I had perjured myself, but I had a very good reason. The four other witnesses for the defence were quite unshakable, and the fact that they had given evidence at the police court naturally impressed the Judge. He told the jury in his summing up that it was far better for the gallows to be cheated of one man than that an innocent man should be hanged for a crime he had not committed – whatever else he may have done, he added. The jury, without retiring, acquitted me. Anne was waiting for me in the corridor. "You're wonderful," she said, as I was led away by another polite inspector, on a charge of perjury. I was accused of falsely stating on oath that I had murdered George Cordwell, when in fact I had not done so. This time I made no magistrate impatient. I said nothing throughout the proceedings at the police court or the Old Bailey except to plead guilty and ask for such leniency as the court saw fit to extend to a first offender. That was two years and three months ago. I've earned full good conduct marks and go out tomorrow. I'm marrying Anne. Charles is dead and has left her all his money – quite a lot, thanks to the policy on George's life. So, on the whole, you may think that I've not done so badly, particularly when I tell you that, as a matter of fact, the evidence I gave on Charles' trial was perfectly true. I did murder George Cordwell.

CHAPTER TWO

Tell Tale

There was silence for a moment after the Professor had finished. Then there was much stamping and clapping. His first lecture was undoubtedly an unqualified success. He held up his hand. "Are there any questions?" he asked. Again there was a short silence. Then somebody said, "Wasn't he wrongly convicted, sir?"

"He pleaded guilty to the charge," replied the Professor, "so he could not be wrongly convicted. But, if you mean was he not innocent of the charge to which he pleaded guilty, the answer is 'yes'. I think, however, that he exercised a wise discretion in pleading guilty. Had he successfully pleaded 'Not Guilty', he would certainly have been charged with perjury committed on his trial for murder, and as the Judge trying him would have known that he had been wrongly acquitted of murder by reason of his perjury, he would have been likely to receive a far heavier sentence. Any further questions?"

"How could he have committed the murder if he was miles away at the time?"

"He was not miles away at the time. He explained correctly how he committed the crime when he first gave evidence, but you will remember that he was an expert at preparing alibis in advance. Before he started out to do the murder he had already made the necessary arrangements with Messrs Hinks, Shorter, Snape and Drew in case of accidents."

The Professor paused for a moment and then he went on, "I am afraid I have not added much to your knowledge of jurisprudence, but at any rate the legal aspect of what I have told you is accurate. So I hope you have learned something. I shall continue this series on Wednesday. Good morning to you."

Amid some applause the Professor left the lecture room. "I enjoyed that," he said to himself, "but whatever made me do it?" He had found no answer to his question by the time he was back in his rooms.

Meanwhile the news of his extraordinary lecture was spreading quickly, and it soon reached the ears of the Law Faculty. Although surprised and amused, no one was much perturbed about it. It was obviously the latest American method of advertising. Not a bad idea, either. By the next lecture he would really have the attention of his audience. He would then start properly on his subject. He would probably break out again into a story a little later to keep the interest from flagging. It was unusual, no doubt, but no one worried about it – except the Professor himself.

His next lecture was on Roman law and was fixed for the following day. He arrived at the lecture room in some trepidation, wondering what he would say. He found a tremendous audience awaiting him. It was difficult to believe that there were so many students of Roman law in the University. The room was packed, with many standing, and some sitting on the floor. The truth was that half of his audience were reading mathematics, classics, geography or history, but the good news had spread quickly and they were all law students for the moment. He was greeted with great enthusiasm. "I *will* give them Roman law," he said to himself, but the next that he remembered hearing himself say was, "And so, ladies and gentlemen, I consider that the teaching of Roman law these days is a pure waste of time and I further consider that there is a time and place for everything, and that this is neither the time nor the place for a lecture on so unromantic a subject. Instead, here is a simple story with no moral which should not tax the intellect of any of you."

And he began "Tell Tale."

Tell Tale

There were only two of us in the first-class carriage until a few moments before the train started. Then a young man – little more than a boy – jumped in. The train moved off and we all retired into our papers. We were strangers to one another and it appeared that none of us wanted to talk. However, after the first stop at X, which was two hours' journey from the start, the young man and I exchanged papers and the other occupant – a middle-aged man of nondescript appearance – entered into a desultory sort of conversation with me. After another half-hour or so we stopped at Y and an inspector entered the carriage. Two of us produced first-class tickets but the boy produced none. "I didn't have time to get a ticket," he explained. "I'm going to London."

"Where from?" queried the inspector.

"X," said the boy unblushingly.

"Two pounds one shilling," said the inspector.

"I didn't think it was as much," said the boy. "I'll go third for the rest of the journey. How much will that be?"

ʾaking a few calculations when the
ȝot on at the terminus," he said, "

ᴅ his calculations. "Is that correct?"
ed at his accuser and went red in the
for the moment. Then mumbling, "I
ething else which I took to be his
ᴏ had given him away, he started

," said the inspector. "I shall have
ᴅ I shall want your name and
ch obliged, sir, if you will let me
l to the informer.

ʳe is my card," said the latter.

replied the inspector. "I hope
you." He then took particulars
from the boy, warned him that he would be reported for a
summons, and guided him to a third-class compartment.

The train moved off. We sat in silence. "Suppose you
think that was pretty mean?" said my companion.

"I don't feel called upon to express an opinion," said I.

"Thought you didn't like it," he went on. "Care to know
why I did it?"

"If you think it requires an explanation," I said, "by all
means let me have it."

"Good," said the other. "Put your paper down. It'll take
some time."

"I shouldn't have thought it required long," I said with
some surprise in my voice. "I imagine that you are one of
those highly principled gentlemen who have never done
anything wrong in their lives and who delight in showing
up the sins of others."

"Quite wrong," he replied. "I'm quite unprincipled. I'm
almost incapable of telling the truth. Have been all my

21

life. That's why I did it. Wanted to save him from being what I am. Just a chance it may have that effect. Wish someone had done it for me."

I was not expecting this attitude and was intrigued. "It will be the story of your life, I suppose?" I said, putting down my paper.

"Not the whole of it," he said, "but enough to point the moral. I've always lived on lies. Thrived on them sometimes. But they don't pay in the end, as I found out. Pleasant-looking boy that. Perhaps he'll be more careful in future. Hope so. Boring you?"

"Not yet," I said.

"I was taught to lie by my mother," he began. "Not deliberately, of course. The usual tale. I found she whopped me if I told the truth when I'd been naughty. So I tried lying. She whopped me just the same sometimes; but, on the whole, not so often. So it was worth it. Same at school. A good lie and you might get away with it. Went into business when I left school. Found the cashier was robbing the till. Watched for my opportunity and then made a nice little haul and put the blame on her. You know the idea."

"I understand what you mean," I said.

"Well, after that, one way or another, I improved my financial position until I'd enough to try my luck at Monte Carlo. There I met an attractive young woman, who helped me spend the money which I didn't lose at the tables. The time came when I was down to my last few pounds. Something had to be done about it. I did something. D'you know Monte Carlo?"

"Only on the cinema."

"Well, you may have noticed even there a hawk-eyed gentleman called the Chef, who watches the play all the time on behalf of the Casino. In the event of a dispute between the bank and a player, or between players, he is nearly always able to give a decision because he's seen what happened. If there's a doubt about the matter the Casino pays. I made a simple plan. I gave my girl friend a few instructions and sat down at the roulette table where I usually played. After I had been there about half an hour there was a piercing scream, and my girl friend was carried from the room in what appeared to be a dead faint. Naturally everyone looked to see what had happened. Then the croupier spun the wheel. The result was seven red. The lady sitting next to me had put a substantial bet on it. As the croupier counted her winnings I stretched out my hand in a nonchalant manner to collect them. 'But they're mine,' said the lady. She spoke in French, but I wasn't sure if you'd understand. 'You are mistaken, madam,' I replied politely but very firmly. Then I turned to the Chef and said, 'Monsieur le Chef, you can doubtless assure the lady that the stake was mine.' He was in a difficulty. His attention, like that of everyone else, had been distracted by my screaming girl friend. So had the croupier's. After a short discussion he ordered the croupier to pay us both, and I made six thousand francs. In those days the franc was twenty-five to the pound. I put five thousand francs away and gambled with the balance. My luck was in and I made a lot of money. Once again I had lied my way to success. So far, I suppose, you think I am the last man to be entitled to give that boy away. You're quite right. But you haven't heard the whole story. Just see how I landed up as a result of my capacity for telling lies. I married my girl friend soon after that episode, and bought quite a prosperous little business in London. All went well for a time, but, as my wife's charms faded, I began to seek entertainment elsewhere. She did not always believe my excuses, but I didn't mind very much. Then, one day, she poisoned herself, but I didn't mind that very much. That is to say, I didn't mind it very much at first. After the inquest had started, however, I began to mind a bit more. I'd realised, of course, that a husband – particularly an unfaithful one – is liable to be suspected if his wife dies an unnatural death. But my consciousness of complete innocence in the matter had prevented me from worrying. I lied, of course, to the police when I was asked a few questions about my relationship with my wife. Said we were a devoted couple and that I had no outside interests. I lied more from habit than otherwise. Unfortunately, however, one of my outside interests, a temporary blonde – temporary in all senses as far as I was concerned – spoke to the coroner's officer about me. Having lied to the police I thought I'd better stick to the same story, and I lied to the coroner too. Said I didn't know the lady. It was just my luck that I'd written her one letter. Nothing in it – but it showed I knew her. The press began to take an interest in the case. My picture appeared in the papers. One or two more of my discarded outside interests gave information to the police. I stuck to my guns and lied again. Of course, the next I knew was that I was charged with murder. I at once employed a solicitor. I told him how ludicrous the charge was, but I didn't quite like the way he agreed with me. I told the magistrate how absurd it all was, and he said, in effect, that I could tell that to the jury at the Old Bailey. And to the Old Bailey I went. Naturally I wasn't pleased about it, but knowing I was innocent and having a great faith in British justice I wasn't unduly alarmed. My counsel told me that the case against me wasn't overwhelming but that it was a pity I'd told so many lies. That was the difficulty, he said. And believe me it was. Unless you're a liar in a big way you can have no idea of the trouble you can get yourself into in the witness box when you try to lie yourself out of inconsistent lies. I can tell you, I was covered with sweat when I'd finished in the box. I still wasn't too apprehensive about the verdict, but I had a very gruelling day and the Judge and prosecuting counsel had a high old time with me. There's no doubt I was forced to tell a good many inconsistent stories. However, I began to feel uncomfortable only when I heard the closing speeches. The case against me, as put by counsel for the prosecution, seemed rather too convincing. The case for me, as put by my own counsel, seemed to lack something. At the close of his speech I asked the Judge for permission to speak. 'It is unusual,' he said, 'but, as this is a case of murder, tell me what you want to say.' I then said that I freely admitted that I was a consummate liar and that I wanted the Judge and jury to know that I'd told lies all my life. It was only telling lies which had put me in the dock. But that didn't mean I was a murderer. 'Very well,' said the Judge, 'the jury have heard what you say.' He then proceeded to sum up. It was not, I suppose, an unfair summing up, but it didn't sound at all good to me. Among other things he said this: 'Members of the jury, the accused has told you that he is a liar. No one who heard his evidence would be disposed to disagree with him on that point. He has also said, quite rightly, that he is being tried for murder, not for telling lies. But what you have to ask yourselves is, why should he tell those lies? Why should an innocent man involve himself in such a way? What could he gain from such a course of conduct? The prosecution say that the different and conflicting stories told by the accused are consistent only with his having something to hide – that is, the murder of his wife. It is for you to judge, members of the jury, whether those comments are well founded.'

"The jury judged all right. They found me guilty. I was thunderstruck. Even when I'd started to become a bit anxious I couldn't really believe that I could be convicted of a crime I'd had nothing to do with. 'My Lord,' I said, when the clerk asked me if I'd anything to say, 'this is terrible. I'm absolutely innocent. What can I do about it?'

" 'You can appeal,' said his Lordship, 'to the Court of Criminal Appeal. Meantime it is my duty to pass sentence of death upon you,' and this he proceeded to do. I duly appealed and was present in court when the appeal was heard. My counsel spoke for an hour and then the Judges conferred together for a few minutes. When they'd finished conferring, I heard the Lord Chief Justice start to give judgment. 'The only reason this appeal is brought,' he said, 'is because it is a case of murder.'

" 'That seems a pretty good reason,' I put in.

" 'If you interrupt again,' said the Judge calmly, 'you will be removed.' He then went on to finish his judgment, which ended with the words 'accordingly the appeal fails and will be dismissed.'

"I was now, as you will understand, pretty frantic. I don't suppose you've been charged with a crime of which you knew you were innocent."

"I have never been charged at all," I said.

"Quite so," he went on. "Well, you can't imagine the hell I went through. I wrote screeds and screeds to the Home Secretary and anyone else I could think of. Heaven knows what I said. I was almost beside myself. Eventually the Governor sent for me. 'The Home Secretary is unable to advise a reprieve in your case,' he said.

" 'That means I'm going to be hanged?' I asked.

" 'Yes,' said the Governor. At that I broke down, I don't know what I did or said and I next remember being in my cell again."

He shivered slightly, as though living through the agony afresh. Then he went on, "Well – I hope it taught that boy a lesson anyway," and relapsed into silence.

"But what happened? How did you get a reprieve in the end?" I asked.

"I never was reprieved."

"But," I began.

"I know – I know," he said. "You want to know why I'm here now. It's quite simple really. I'm an incorrigible liar."

CHAPTER THREE

Slander

There was considerable applause at the end of the Professor's story. As before, he asked if there were any questions.

"I guessed it was going to finish like that," said a girl student.

"That was very clever of you," said the Professor, "as I didn't know myself what the end was going to be until I got there."

"Are many innocent people convicted in England?" asked another.

"In serious matters I should say very few indeed, if any," replied the Professor. "Nothing in the world is perfect, but it is a principle of English law that it is better for a hundred guilty men to be acquitted than for one innocent man to be convicted. To draw on my own personal recollection, while I was at the Bar, I think I appeared for half a dozen people who were acquitted, but I am tolerably certain that none of them was innocent."

"Do you mean to say that you appeared for men whom you believed to be guilty?" the Professor was asked almost immediately.

"Most decidedly so," was his reply. "What has my belief got to do with it? It is for the jury or magistrate to say if a man is guilty. If a barrister had to believe in his client's innocence in order to enable him to act as his counsel, most accused persons would lose the right of being defended at all. Oh dear me, yes. An advocate must not put forward what he positively knows to be a false case. Nevertheless he is quite entitled and, indeed, he is usually bound to put forward his client's defence, however little he believes in it, provided only he does not know for certain that it is untrue. Dr Johnson had some very sensible things to say on the subject. I would refer you to him if you wish to go deeper into the matter. Now, if there are no further questions, I should like to make an announcement to my class in Roman law. Will everyone else please withdraw." The room emptied and the Professor was left with the dozen young men who made up his class.

"Gentlemen," said the Professor, "when we last met in my rooms I neglected to give you the subject for the weekly essay. I should like you to let me have about one thousand words on 'The Gift in Roman Law.' Let me have them by midday tomorrow, please. That is all, thank you." His pupils left and the Professor started back for his rooms. "I've done it again," he said to himself. "Now, why on earth?"

The news of his first lecture on Roman law spread equally quickly. The Law Faculty was still not unduly worried. The first of each series, it said to itself. However, it decided to send a representative to the second lecture on jurisprudence on the next day. This is what the representative heard. "I dealt in my opening lecture, ladies and gentlemen, with the juridical conceptions of right and wrong. I did that deliberately. No doubt most of you had expected an introduction to the study of jurisprudence, but I have always found it more satisfactory to reserve that for the second lecture. I prefer to interest you in my subject before I describe what it is."

"Exactly what we thought," said the representative of the Law Faculty to himself. "There's nothing wrong at all."

"Now what is jurisprudence? What do we mean by the word? I will pause for a moment for you to think out an answer among yourselves and then I will continue." There was a murmur of disappointment among an audience which had been expecting something very different. The mathematical and other intruder students wondered how they could get out in the middle without making themselves too obvious. As they comprised at least half the audience it was quite impossible. "Very well," continued the Professor, "jurisprudence. What is it? A lot of bunkum, ladies and gentlemen, a lot of hooey." The representative of the Law Faculty sat up with a jerk. "Bunkum. Hooey," repeated the Professor. "You haven't come here to hear that sort of twaddle, have you? Of course not. This time I will tell you a story with a moral. I hope you will profit by it."

Slander

None of us in the mess liked Bogg. He was a solicitor, but it was not just that. An unassuming and well-behaved solicitor is an asset to any mess. Unfortunately Bogg had neither of these qualities. He would loudly disagree with senior officers in terms which suggested that their education had been sadly neglected. This may have been true, but it was not for Bogg to say so. Then, again, without the slightest provocation he would launch into a discussion about some aspect of the law or the legal profession. Invariably on these occasions he would manage to bring in some experience of his own and explain how he had worsted his opponents by his consummate skill. As a regular officer I naturally have a high opinion of lawyers, but Bogg's methods seemed to me to savour of low cunning and to be unworthy of a great profession. I did not say so, because, although I was a major and Bogg only a subaltern, he invariably got the better of me in any argument. I did not like to be reduced to the method adopted by our Colonel, who would simply say, "Be quiet, Bogg," when he could think of no better answer to Bogg's last point. Bogg was, of course, in great demand at Courts Martial. The soldiers did not realise that the only effect of his pettifogging ways was to make the court certain to convict, and to incline it to pass a more severe sentence than it would otherwise have considered appropriate. His military clients always felt that everything possible had been done for them and recommended him to their friends. If the average member of the public is as gullible as the average soldier it is not surprising that solicitors of the Bogg variety can flourish.

Bogg had been with us in North Africa for about six months when he made a remark which excited no interest at the time, but which some of us recalled vividly later. The Colonel had spoken disparagingly of some public man, when Bogg piped up with "If I may say so, sir, that is a very dangerous remark to make, unless you can prove your facts. You might easily be sued for slander if there were a friend of his here."

"Be quiet, Bogg," said the Colonel, and the incident closed and would have been forgotten but for subsequent events.

Well, the war finished and I retired from the Army on pension, and so did the Colonel. Others, including Bogg, went back to their civilian jobs. Several of us continued to keep in touch, but naturally Bogg dropped out of our lives. One day I was surprised to receive a visit from the Colonel. It was the first time he had called without at least telephoning first. I could see at once that he was worried. I had been his second-in-command and he had been accustomed to discuss his difficulties with me, so I could tell when he was upset. He did not waste words. "Look at this," he said, and showed me a letter. It was from a firm of solicitors, Bogg, Tewkesbury and Co., and read as follows:

"Lt Col D A Browne,
The Red House,
Birsted.

DEAR SIR,

We have been consulted by our client, Miss Euterpe Onapoulos of Alexandria. Our client has for some time past been the victim of a cruel attack upon her moral character. Utterly baseless rumours as to our client's mode of life have been circulating in Alexandria and the neighbourhood, and, in view of our client's profession of a teacher, they have naturally done her incalculable harm. Our client has been trying for some time to trace the source of these rumours, and in the course of doing so she communicated with us. It so happened that our Mr Bogg was present in the officers' mess of the 8th Blankshires, then stationed just outside Alexandria, on an occasion when you used highly defamatory words about our client, clearly suggesting that she was a woman of immoral character. If you wish to be reminded of the exact words you used, we will, of course, set them on record, but they were coarsely expressed and could not be dictated to a lady typist. If this matter goes to court they will have to be repeated verbatim, but we hope in everyone's interests that this will not be necessary. Our client is not in a position to prove that the subsequent rumours about her character originated from the slander you published, but we think it extremely likely that this was the case. However that may be, our client hopes that by making an example of you it may be possible to stamp out the slanders once and for all.

Our client has no wish to derive any pecuniary benefit from this malicious attack upon her, but she is determined to re-establish and protect her good name. Accordingly she requires you to offer forthwith an unqualified apology and to agree to its publication in all Egyptian papers at your expense. At the same time, in order to mark the occasion and as a warning to others, she requires you to pay the sum of £100 to the Egyptian Maternity Hospital. You will also be required to pay our costs in the matter.

If you are not prepared to comply with our client's extremely reasonable demands, please let us have the name and address of solicitors who will accept service of a writ on your behalf."

Before I could comment on this letter he handed me another, which he told me had arrived separately by the same post. It was headed "without prejudice" and read as follows:

"DEAR COLONEL,

I am so sorry about this Euterpe Onapoulos business, but I did warn you once about saying things of other people! Anyway, I think I could settle the whole thing for you for £25. My client is a difficult young woman, but, as you were my CO, I would put in a good word for you. I do strongly advise you to settle the case at once, as the lady is determined on taking action if you don't. However, don't take my advice – go to your own solicitors and I'm sure they'll tell you you'd be a fool not to. It seems funny talking to you like this, but I'm sure you don't mind. What a long time it seems since the old days.

YOURS SINCERELY,

GEORGE ('BE QUIET') BOGG."

I was very fond of the Colonel and my heart went out to him when I thought of his feelings on reading that second letter. His blood pressure was a little high when he retired and I was relieved to find he had stood the shock so well. His face was only very red and not purple, and he was able to speak coherently. "Do you remember any Euterpe What's-her-name?" he asked me.

"Never heard of her," I said. "Of course, there were one or two Greek young ladies who interested some of the subalterns, but I never knew their names."

"Will you come with me to my solicitors?" he said.

I agreed, and the same day we made an appointment with Mr Pearson of Pearson, Jogworth and Hansome – a most respectable firm. The Colonel showed Mr Pearson the letters and told him all he knew. "Can you be certain," said Mr Pearson, "that you have never spoken lightly of a lady in the mess?"

"How can I be certain?" said the Colonel.

"I was afraid you couldn't be," said Mr Pearson. "Now this is the position," he went on. "It is possible that Miss Euterpe Onapoulos exists only in the imagination of Mr Bogg – but I doubt this. If his bluff were called and the truth discovered, he could be ruined. Bogg, Tewkesbury and Co. is not a very reputable firm, but I doubt whether he would risk as much as that for £25. We must, therefore, assume that the lady does exist. It is probable that from time to time in your mess some subaltern has, quite contrary I believe to the proper etiquette, boasted of his exploits with a lady in Alexandria. Comment by other officers – possibly including yourself – has followed, not always to the credit of the lady. If Mr Bogg were to give evidence that on one occasion a lady whom he knew to be Miss Onapoulos was mentioned in the mess and that you made some disparaging remark about her, you would probably be unable to deny the fact. It may well be that, if Miss Onapoulos does exist, she is no better than she ought to be, and inquiry into the subjects which she teaches might prove interesting. Such inquiries, however, would cost much more than £25. Moreover, even if they proved conclusively that she deserved the reputation she alleges that she has acquired, you would not recover from her anything like the amount spent by you in fighting the case. In consequence, whether you win or lose, you will be out of pocket by several hundred pounds. Mr Bogg has made you a tempting offer. If you take my advice you will accept it quickly before he raises his price. I will, if you prefer it, compel him to issue a writ and see whether he really has a client – but, as I have said, I don't think he would dare invent the whole thing. He may easily have persuaded Miss Onapoulos to act the part, but this you would only be able to prove, if at all, by bringing the action to trial, which, as I have said, would be an extremely expensive proceeding."

"It is just pure blackmail," said the Colonel. "Outrageous, abominable, and scandalous," he added.

"It is everything you say," said Mr Pearson, "but you will be out of it cheaply for £25. Your wisest course is to leave the matter in my hands and authorise me to settle it as best I can – expending altogether a maximum of £50."

After some further expostulation the Colonel finally agreed, and I had to admit it seemed the only course to take. Actually, in the end, it cost him (including his own solicitors' costs) £44 10s 6d. Bogg had certainly had his revenge.

A few weeks later I was rung up by Arthur Galley, our late Adjutant, who asked if he could come and see me. I agreed, and he came the same day. As soon as we'd exchanged greetings, he came straight to the point. "You remember Bogg?" he said. I did – and I also remembered that Mr Bogg had more than once suffered at the hands of our Adjutant. Arthur was a man of few words, but they were, when necessary, sharp – extremely sharp. In Bogg's case it had often been necessary. I guessed what was coming.

"You've had a letter from Messrs Bogg, Tewkesbury and Co.," I said.

"How did you know?" he asked.

So I told him all about the Colonel. Arthur Galley said a few very sharp words. He had received two somewhat similar letters. The first made complaints on behalf of a Mr Ahmed Ali, a grocer in Alexandria, whose reputation as a trader Galley was alleged to have impugned. I have no doubt he had. The gentleman in question charged the most extortionate prices, and his name was a by-word in the mess for robbery without violence. The letter made demands for apologies and £100, to be paid to the Egyptian Traders' Welfare Association. The letter from Bogg himself was in the following terms:

"Without prejudice

"DEAR OLD BOY" – (he had never dared call Arthur anything but 'sir', even in the mess),

"It's an awful shame worrying you like this. I know how busy you must be – if you work anything like as hard as you did when Adjutant. I often used to think you overdid it. However, enough of that. I can help you to settle this claim for £30 probably, if you're quick in answering. Go along to your own solicitors, old boy – don't take it from me, but you'll be more of a blithering idiot than ever if you don't take the chance. How are things? I love to think of the old days sometimes, don't you, old boy?

So long,

Yours,

GEORGE."

We went to Arthur's solicitors. Their advice was very much the same as in the Colonel's case. They pointed out that we all knew there was a Mr Ahmed Ali and that the only question was whether Bogg had received any instructions from him at all. Again they doubted if he would take the risk of acting without instructions. They were very sympathetic and would, of course, be only too pleased to fight the case if Arthur preferred, but in their view £30 was a cheap get-out. In the end it cost him £65. I rather fancied that the advice the Adjutant had sometimes given Bogg would cost him more than the Colonel's moderate "Be quiet, Bogg."

I was not in the least surprised when, a few weeks later, Bogg's late Company Commander came to see me with a similar tale of woe. It cost him £80. I began to wonder when it would be my turn, and I was rather relieved to think that I had always treated Bogg rather better than most people. I did not remember having snubbed him, and I never spoke to him at all if it wasn't absolutely necessary.

When, however, the padre and the doctor received the usual letters, I felt that something must be done about it. I arranged a conference of all the victims at my house. I put forward my plan; it was enthusiastically adopted and immediately acted upon.

Some weeks later I received a very polite letter from Messrs Bogg, Tewkesbury and Co. It read as follows:

"DEAR SIR,

We understand that you were in the same battalion as our Mr Bogg during the last war, and we would be extremely grateful if you can give us your assistance. Mr Bogg has received a letter from Messrs Groaner and Groaner, solicitors for a Major Skipton, complaining that, on an occasion in the mess during the last war, Mr Bogg suggested that Major Skipton had been guilty of dishonest dealings in regard to RASC supplies. It is alleged that these words were heard by the then Commanding Officer, the Adjutant and certain other officers.

Mr Bogg cannot understand the allegation, as not only was he unaware of Major Skipton's existence (though he has since observed his name in the Army List), but he never spoke in the least disparagingly of any officer or indeed of any person. He was, in fact, especially careful not to associate himself with those who were less particular as to their remarks in the mess. Accordingly, we should be very much obliged if you could tell us anything which might throw some light on the matter. Possibly our client was mistaken for someone else. The actual words alleged to have been spoken by Mr Bogg are 'That old fox Skipton makes a good thing out of his job. I bet his family are never short of rations, but the old skinflint wouldn't even give me a tin of margarine – he ought to get seven years.'

An early reply would greatly oblige."

This was my answer:

"DEAR SIRS,
Thank you for your letter. I think I can assist you in the matter. I well remember an occasion when Mr Bogg spoke of Major Skipton. Mr Bogg has, no doubt, forgotten that Major Skipton was in charge of a DID near our Battalion HQ. Mr Bogg was about to go on leave, and he told us that he had met Major Skipton and asked him whether he could let him have some tea and sugar. I do not remember the margarine, but he may have asked for this too. Apparently his request was refused and Mr Bogg said very much what appears in your letter. I naturally do not remember the exact words. For example, I cannot recollect the word 'fox' being used. I think it was 'scoundrel', but I may be wrong. I particularly remember the occasion, as, in view of Mr Bogg's warnings to the members of the mess, I was amazed at his talking like that. In fact I said, 'Aren't you afraid of being sued for slander?' to which he replied, 'I can something well prove it.' I will supply the word he used where I have put 'something' if you wish. If there is any further assistance I can give Mr Bogg, please let me know."

I then wrote a letter to Bogg himself.

"DEAR BOGG" (I wrote),
    "I am very sorry indeed to hear of your misfortunes. They seem to be catching in our battalion. You probably don't know, but the CO, Adjutant and your late Company Commander have all had to pay up a total of just on £190. The padre and the doctor have each been stung for £25. I realise, of course, that theirs were only trifling cases

compared with yours, and I am not surprised that you are concerned about it. After all, they are only laymen, and a few words spoken in haste by a mere soldier can't be as harmful as a deliberate statement made by a well-known and experienced lawyer. I happen to have kept in touch with Major Skipton, and if I can help you to settle the matter I should be only too pleased to do so. I believe he would take £250, if you offered it to him at once, but if you make him go into court I'm sure he'll want a lot more. Let me know if I can help."

I then went to Messrs Groaner & Groaner who, curiously enough, treated me as though I were Major Skipton. I told them I would settle for £250. Bogg squealed and wriggled, but there were five or six potential witnesses against him (I was not quite sure about the padre) and, eventually, after several interviews between the solicitors, he settled the matter for £250. This was duly re-distributed among Bogg's victims, and with the balance (less one shilling) we all had dinner at the Savoy (including the padre).

The Colonel insisted on spending the shilling on a telegram. The text of this ran: "Be quiet, Bogg." And he was.

CHAPTER FOUR

On Principle

Immediately at the end of the story the representative from the Law Faculty slipped out. Something must be done about it. He duly made his report and it was decided to let the Master of St James' have a word with the Professor. The latter had meanwhile dealt with a fairly large number of questions. After that, he collected the essays from his Roman law class and started back for his rooms.

"I don't understand it at all," he said to himself, "but they seem to like it all right." He reached St James' and found a note asking him to go and see the Master. He went to the Lodge at once. The Master was waiting for him and was obviously ill at ease. Eventually, after a little normal conversation, he said, "Are you feeling quite all right?"

"Perfectly, thank you," said the Professor.

"I seem to remember your mentioning that you bumped your head on arrival at the station."

"Yes – I did, but it's quite all right again, thank you. Why do you ask?" The Master was not finding the interview very easy – but it had got to be done.

"Your lectures," he said. "How are they going?"

"Splendidly, thank you. Absolutely packed out."

41

"I didn't quite mean that. Have you been delivering your normal lectures on each subject?" The Professor hesitated. Then he said, "It's rather curious that you should ask that, because I haven't. How did you know?"

"I've had a report about them."

"To what effect?"

"Well – I know it sounds absurd – but I've been told that you've simply been telling stories – in a legal setting, it's true – but stories which have no relation whatever to jurisprudence or Roman law."

"It's extraordinary, isn't it?" said the Professor. "I'm glad you've raised the subject because I wanted to mention it to someone, but felt a little uncomfortable about doing so."

"What is the trouble?"

"Well – you've said it sounds absurd, and it is absurd. I go to the lecture room prepared to deliver my normal lecture, and, to my amazement, I find myself quite unable to do so. Instead I hear a voice exactly like mine – and, of course, I know it is mine, but it sounds as though it comes from someone else's body – telling a story. I can assure you that I have got up to start, absolutely determined to lecture on one of my subjects, only to find myself completely unable to do so."

"I'm terribly sorry," said the Master. "I expect you've had a rare type of concussion. We'll get Murray to have a look at you. I'm afraid it may mean going into a – into a nursing home for a week or two. But we'll see what he says about it. I can't tell you how sorry I am. It is very bad luck. However, I expect Murray will be able to throw some light on it. Now, let's have some lunch."

The same afternoon the Professor kept an appointment with Dr Murray, an eminent psychiatrist, and Dr Spencer, a consulting physician. After a careful physical examination by Dr Spencer, the psychiatrist made the usual inquiries as to the Professor's past history and took down very full notes. He was really interested in the case. It was something quite new. At the end he said, "Now there's nothing to worry about at all, Professor. I want to impress that on you. There is nothing physically wrong with you at all. On the other hand, it would be silly of me to say that I knew what was the matter. We'll have to keep you under observation for a short time, and I'm sure at the end of it we'll have the answer. Now there's a very nice nursing home not far from here and I'd like you to go into it."

"But, if there's nothing wrong with me physically, why should I stay in bed?"

"Bed? Oh, certainly not. You'll be able to do just what you like. It's a charming house with lovely grounds and I'm sure you'll enjoy it. I realise what a nuisance it must be for you just at the start of the term, but I'm sure it will be best."

"Very well," sighed the Professor. "I suppose you know what's good for me – and I certainly would like to find out what is the matter."

"Good. Then I'll make all the arrangements. When would you like to go?"

"As soon as possible, if I'm going at all. I want to get back to my work."

"Quite right. Well, I can get you in this afternoon. You might drive over there about teatime. It's only about fifty miles away."

"Very well," said the Professor. "Thank you very much. I'll go and get ready."

He went back to his rooms in a rather uncertain frame of mind, but, on the whole, glad that his extraordinary experiences were going to be investigated. He packed his things, handed over the essays he had collected to another law tutor at St James', and by teatime he was on his way to Tapworth House, which was the name of the home.

The tutor to whom he handed the essays was a much younger man. His name was Williams and he had a good deal of the schoolmaster in him. He was in consequence rather inclined to treat undergraduates as though they were still at school. Although the behaviour of some of them is quite consistent with this being the case, it is, on the whole, an unwise approach to the boy who has just grown up. In due course Dr Williams (he was an LLD) read the essays which had been handed to him by the Professor. He read them without much enthusiasm. "The Gift in Roman Law" is not a subject which lends itself to interesting treatment. At length, however, he came to the essay by Mr George Pringle, and, when he had read it, he asked Mr Pringle to come and see him. Mr Pringle was nineteen and very full of life. He was not a particularly studious young man, although he read a fair amount for pleasure. His reading, however, was confined to subjects which interested him (and Roman law was not one) or to light fiction.

"Mr Pringle," said Dr Williams, "Professor Melton is ill and I am taking his class instead."

Mr Pringle started to go red in the face and to shift uneasily from one foot to the other.

"Oh – yes, sir," he said. " I'm very sorry."

"I thought you probably would be," said Dr Williams. "But tell me, in your own words, why are you so sorry?"

"I'm always sorry for anyone who's ill and I liked the Professor."

"You hadn't known him for more than two or three days."

"No, sir, but I like and dislike very quickly."

"Indeed? And is there no other reason you are sorry for his departure?"

Mr Pringle did not answer.

"Let me suggest one," said Dr Williams. "Did you write an essay for the Professor?"

"Well – yes – I did, sir."

"What was the subject he gave you?"

"The Gift in Roman Law."

"Is this your handwriting?"

"It seems to be, sir."

"Well, you must know whether it is or is not."

"It is, sir."

"Very well, I have selected your essay for reading out to the class this evening."

"That's very gratifying, sir."

"I hope the Master will be able to be present."

"D'you think he'd like it, sir?"

"We shall see, when it's read. I will keep it for the moment and hand it to you when you come with the others. That's all, thank you." Mr Pringle left.

"I don't care," he said to himself. All the same he felt considerably embarrassed a few hours later when Dr Williams, after some preliminary remarks, said: "Mr Pringle will now read his essay on 'The Gift in Roman Law.'"

"You really want me to read it, sir?" said Mr Pringle.

"That is why I asked you," said Dr Williams.

"Very well, then," said Mr Pringle. "As I've been told to read it, I will. But I do ask you all, particularly you, Master, when you are considering its merits, to bear in mind the lecture which Professor Melton delivered before he gave out the subject to us. You may find that I have been influenced by his style." The Master looked at Dr Williams, but Dr Williams avoided his eye, and this is what Mr Pringle read:

On Principle

I am a young lady lying in bed in an hotel. I am not a very good young lady, but, then again, I am not a very bad young lady. I think you would find me a satisfactory mixture. I'm sure you find really good young people terribly boring and really bad ones almost worse. I am tantalisingly between the two and I think we should get on very well together – provided, of course, that you are also neither one thing nor the other, and provided, too, that you have pleasant manners and are quite good looking. I am talking naturally to young men. Young women will not be interested in me.

Ever since I was a child the good and bad in me have taken it in turns. For instance, when I was naughty in the morning I would try and make up for it in the afternoon by being particularly good. I did the same at school. If I was admonished for making a noise while we were supposed to be working, I would try to do a specially good exercise afterwards. I would really take trouble over it. So, again, when I took my first job, if I arrived at the office after nine o'clock in the morning I would stay on during the lunch hour or go home late. Always I have felt the necessity for making up for what I had done wrong. You will probably call it conscience. I don't care for that word but prefer to talk of my behaviour as acting in accordance with my principles.

The other evening I, this not very good and not very bad young lady, was lying in bed, just as I am now, glancing at a book and wondering whether I should be happier at the dance downstairs. Suddenly the door of my room opened and a man came in quickly, shutting the door behind him very quietly. As soon as he saw me he took out a revolver. Then he spoke: "Please not to make scream. I not speak English well, but this" (and he indicated the revolver) "speak for me in each language."

"Nonsense," I said, "you speak perfect English. I heard you in the bus this afternoon. And do put down that ridiculous thing."

"Oh – all right," he said, "I didn't know we'd met before."

"We haven't," I said, "but I recognised you from seeing you in the bus this afternoon. Do put it down. I am a poor defenceless girl. You don't need a revolver to deal with me."

"Suppose you ring the bell?" he said.

"Well, there is that, I admit," I answered, "but I'll promise not to ring it for ten minutes if you'll put that away. It makes you look so hideous. I must say you looked quite nice in the bus – from the short glance I took at you."

"Very well," he said, and put the revolver in his pocket. "Good," I said, "now would you like to tell me why you are honouring me with a visit? But do sit down first."

He sat down in a chair and gave a sigh. "I'm just a hotel thief."

"Well, I'm afraid I haven't very much for you. Now I believe the lady next door …"

He interrupted. "I didn't come to get anything from you. A porter was after me and I slipped in here instead of going downstairs. I've got what I want. I don't know why I'm telling you all this."

"I asked you why you came here," I reminded him. "Do you like being a hotel thief?" I went on.

47

"No," he answered, "but I've got to do something. I've tried almost everything honest from a city clerk down to a gigolo – but I couldn't get on at anything."

"Poor boy," I said. Now that he had put his revolver away he certainly looked very handsome. He ought to have succeeded as a gigolo. I suppose he was too independent. I like men to be independent. He was well made, too, rather like a Guards Officer, not that I know terribly much about Guards Officers.

"Would you like a drink?" I said. "You'll find a bottle of whisky over there. You can give me one, too, if you like. I think I can do with it. The reaction, you know. I hate revolvers."

"It's very kind of you." He got up and, having found the whisky, poured out two glasses and handed me one. "Neat?" he asked.

"A little water – please."

He gave it to me and I noticed that he had very lovely eyes. I could have done with a pair like his myself – though my own are quite passable.

"Well, here's fun," I said, and added, "But I'm not quite sure that fun is the right word in the circumstances. Have you been to prison before?" He started at that – and put his hand quickly to his pocket. Then, when he saw that I hadn't reached for the bell, he withdrew it rather sheepishly.

"The ten minutes isn't up," I assured him.

"Why did you mention prison then?"

"Oh – I just wondered if you'd been inside. I've never had a chat like this with anyone who has."

"No – I haven't yet."

"Well, I shouldn't go, if I were you. I'm told it's most unpleasant."

"I'm not going, if I can help it."

48

"Then why do you take such risks? You're bound to be caught sooner or later."

"What else can I do? I must live. I tell you, I've tried everything of which I'm capable – and I simply can't make the grade in honest jobs. I'm a fool, I suppose. It was the same at school. I got all the colours for games you could think of – but they wouldn't make me a prefect because I couldn't get higher than the lower fourth."

"What did you do after school?"

"The war started soon after I left. So that was all right for six years. Then I went into the City, but I was so stupid that I lost job after job. The time came when I couldn't even get a reference. D'you know, I've even tried selling newspapers and I couldn't make a success of that."

"You certainly have tried," I said, "and you are very good looking."

"Well – I tried to cash in on that too, but I could never get going. I suppose I didn't have enough capital to turn myself out well enough at the start. Then, even when I did get a stroke of luck, I was rude to the customers."

"Oh – that's fatal," I said, "but I admire you for it."

"Finally I took to this. I haven't done too badly so far, but I'm so stupid that I'm bound to be caught soon – in spite of what I said."

"I think it's a shame that anyone looking like you should be reduced to this," I said." I really am terribly sorry for you. I'd like to help."

"What can you do? What can anyone do? If someone could remove the sheep's brains from inside my head and substitute something a bit higher up the scale, that might help. I can't think of anything else."

"It's dreadful," I said. "Stand up, and let me have a look at you." He got up slowly and came towards me. He really was a young Apollo. I hadn't realised as much in the bus.

49

He was quite the most attractive young man I had ever seen. He seemed to read my thoughts.

"You're not too bad yourself," he said. "You see," he added, "that's the clumsy way I used to talk to customers. I could never pay them graceful compliments. Now, if you'd been a customer, I shouldn't have had any difficulty."

"I am a customer," I said.

Two hours later I rang the bell and gave him in charge. He hadn't done anything to annoy me – oh no, not at all – but I'm the hotel detective and you'll remember my principles.

CHAPTER FIVE

The Name

"Is that your own or did you take it out of a magazine, Pringle?" said the Master.

"It was out of a magazine, sir."

"Well, I think you'd better do another one by yourself and let me have it by Friday."

"On what subject, sir? The Gift in Roman Law?"

"Certainly not. Any subject you like. You will, of course, do an essay on the Gift in Roman Law for Dr Williams as well. You would like that tomorrow, Williams, I expect?"

"Yes, Master."

"Very well, then, provided Dr Williams has his essay tomorrow and I have my story by Friday we will consider this incident closed. That is, of course, provided I'm satisfied with the story you produce."

The Master left and Dr Williams continued with the class. He was not sure that everything had gone according to plan. Mr Pringle, however, was extremely worried. He had never written a short story in his life and did not know how to set about it. As soon as the class was over he went to George Manners and asked for help. Manners rather fancied himself as a novelist in the making. "I'll produce you a story," he said. "I've got one here. I've got several in fact. Have a look at them." Mr Pringle read them.

"Not bad, are they?" said Manners. Manners was a friend of Mr Pringle, who – as a tribute to their friendship and for no other reason – replied, "Jolly good. But I'm afraid no one would believe I'd written any of them. I shall have to try and work something out myself. Thanks awfully all the same." Mr Pringle was a little fastidious and was not prepared to submit a story which he did not consider had reasonable merit. He left St James' and started to walk towards King's Parade. On the way he met a girl whom he was getting to know fairly well. Her name was Mary Parsons. She was attractive. Even a more fastidious person than Mr Pringle would have thought so. They went on the river and he confided his difficulty to her.

Meanwhile, the real cause of all the trouble – Professor Melton – had arrived at Tapworth House. He was given a room to himself and shortly after he had unpacked he was interviewed by the resident psychiatrist Dr Long, and the visiting physician. Once again he had to describe his childhood, his parents and his idiosyncrasies. At the end, he was told that his was a most interesting case, and it was hoped that he would be comfortable at Tapworth House. "It would be an excellent idea," said Dr Long, "if you would tell some of your stories in the evening. Possibly, if you try to tell a story, you will find yourself lecturing on jurisprudence."

"That would be rather painful for the other patients, wouldn't it?"

"Not at all, I'm sure they'd be interested. I should advise you strongly to amuse yourself as much as possible while you're here. Get to know the other patients and, whatever you do, don't mope around doing nothing. There are plenty of walks, plenty of books, there's bathing, tennis and croquet."

"I will certainly try to take your advice," said the Professor.

He left the doctors and wandered into the lounge. Immediately he found himself the centre of attraction. Twenty pairs of eyes were focused on him. Some of the owners had books in front of them, some had newspapers, and some had nothing at all, but they turned their eyes on the Professor as one man. It was quite a creditable drill movement. He found a chair as quickly as possible and sat down. Bearing the doctor's advice in mind, he turned to the man who was in the chair next to him and said "Good evening." Mr Wilkins, the man in question, darted a quick look at the Professor before replying. Then he said, "I've been here for six months."

"Oh – indeed," said the Professor, "and what exactly is your trouble?"

At once the eyes, which had allowed themselves to stray from the Professor, became fixed on him again. Instinctively the Professor realised that he had asked the forbidden question. Mr Wilkins darted another quick look at the Professor. "Supper's at eight," he said, and got up and walked out of the room. A bad beginning, thought the Professor. He turned to his other neighbour – a middle-aged man with deep-set staring eyes. "And how long have you been here?" he asked.

"Yes," said his neighbour, "I have. And why not, may I ask?"

"No reason at all," said the Professor, anxious to humour him.

"Then why put the question?"

"I'm sorry," said the Professor. "Please disregard it."

"I will think about it," said his neighbour.

The Professor picked up a magazine, but he did not really read. He was beginning to feel that Tapworth House was not quite what he had expected. He hadn't realised they were all mental cases.

"I don't think I can stand very much of this," he thought. "It would drive me quite mad."

At that moment a maid came into the room. "Supper is ready," she said. She had hardly got the words out of her mouth before everyone in the room, except the Professor, was on his feet and moving as quickly as possible towards the dining-room. Within ten seconds of the maid's arrival the Professor was left alone in the lounge.

"I suppose they have nothing else to think about," he said to himself. He was quite right, and it saved him some further embarrassment. He had expected to have all eyes focused on him again when he entered the dining-room alone, but he was pleased to find that everyone was so engrossed in eating that not the slightest notice was taken of his entrance. He sat down and had his supper and then went back to the lounge. He had been there only a few minutes when Dr Long came in. It struck the Professor that Dr Long and the patients were like a trainer and his performing animals. All eyes were turned on him, but not in the way in which they had been turned on the Professor. This was their master whose every word must be obeyed.

"Good evening, gentlemen," said Dr Long.

"Good evening, Doctor," came the response in chorus.

"As you know, Professor Melton has come to stay with us for a short time, and he's promised to entertain us with one of the delightful talks for which he is so famous."

The eyes remained on the doctor.

"Would you be so kind, Professor?"

"Oh, certainly, if you would like it," said the Professor. "Though I'm not sure that I have anything very – anything that would interest you." He had been going to say "very suitable," but he thought he might be misunderstood.

"I'm sure that any talk from you will be greatly appreciated, Professor," said the doctor.

"Very well, then," said the Professor. "I will tell you a story – not a very long one – and I hope it will amuse you."

As he started, the doctor went out.

The Name

"Put up George Elephant," said the Clerk in Court I of the Old Bailey, and a small bespectacled man was brought up into the dock.

"Are you George Elephant?" asked the Clerk.

"I am."

"You are charged on an indictment containing one count – murder – in that you, at Golders Green on the nineteenth day of January, 1948, murdered Jane Elephant. How say you, George Elephant, are you guilty or not guilty?"

"Not guilty."

"Very well," said the Judge, "you may sit down."

"Thank you, my Lord."

Except for a few comments on the curious name of the prisoner, the case had excited little interest. The facts alleged by the prosecution were very simple. On the 20th January the prisoner had walked into a police station. "I have cut my wife's throat," he said. "She's quite dead." They investigated his statement and it seemed true enough. Her throat had apparently been cut with a razor which was near the body. George was charged with the murder and in due course committed for trial. No defence was put forward at the police court. It seemed a clear case. The prisoner was, however, defended by Sir Gordon Macintosh, KC, who seldom accepted facts at their face value. He never took on more than one case at a time and he went into that case very thoroughly indeed. These are the facts he discovered about George Elephant.

George was born of ordinary middle-class parents at the end of the nineteenth century. There was no trace of insanity in the family. George had had a normal upbringing and had gone into his father's business – quite a prosperous one – on leaving school. Thereafter he had married and settled down to an ordinary normal existence. Jane was not a particularly attractive wife. Although inclined to prettiness she was more inclined, as she grew older, to blowsiness. She would describe herself as a "good sport" and would sometimes say playfully that she was "rather a tease." She certainly derived considerable pleasure from teasing George, and one of the subjects of which she never seemed to get tired was his surname. George was very self-conscious about his name, but he had never had the courage to change it.

I have known a Sidebottom very reasonably change his name to Edgedale when he had grown impatient of practical jokers' telephone calls.

Usually, however, the owners of unfortunate names grin and bear them, or, rather, they bear them while others grin. George undoubtedly had suffered a great deal. When he first went to school and was asked his name in front of the other boys he replied, "George Elephant."

"Olliphant?" said the master.

"No, sir, Elephant."

"What, Elephant? Like the animals in the Zoo?"

"Yes, sir, like the animals in the Zoo."

Thereafter at school he was called by the name of all known and some unknown animals. George was inclined to be shy, and boys at school are merciless. He was not happy there and was thankful when he left. His troubles did not end when he left school, however. Like Mr Sidebottom, he received many calls from the people who have nothing better to do than to use the telephone as a means of annoyance.

"Is that Mr Elephant?" "Yes." "Would you like a new trunk, by any chance?"

Or, "Is that Mr Elephant?" "Yes." "How are the tusks today?"

You Smiths and Robinsons, who have never suffered in this way, may smile and make light of these unwelcome attentions from unmannerly strangers, but change your name to Rabbit-Pie or Unicorn – even for a fortnight – and see what happens to you. Some of the Elephant family did, in fact, change their name to Olliphant, but George's father said that what was good enough for his father was good enough for him and stuck resolutely to Elephant. George, indeed, had no pride in his name, but, for no precise reason, he shrank from changing it. So he suffered – not gladly, but because he was powerless to do otherwise – the smiles of the shopgirls when he gave his name and the continual jibes of the telephone joker. He even thought of giving up the telephone, but the inconvenience he would suffer from the loss of a telephone, and a certain stubbornness, prevented him. When he married Jane he had hoped that he would have a partner to share and make lighter his difficulties. Jane, however, was not in the least self-conscious at being called Jane Elephant; on the contrary, she paraded the fact, whenever she had the chance, particularly if her husband was near. Even when she was being affectionate she would call him "my elephant boy," and so it happened that, even in their most tender moments, he was not allowed to forget. When Sir

Gordon Macintosh had discovered these facts he had no doubt at all as to the proper defence to raise. He immediately had George examined by eminent psychiatrists and advised that they should give evidence at the trial on his behalf. He notified the prosecution that he intended to adopt this course, and consequently they also had George examined by more psychiatrists. The defence which Sir Gordon put forward was in the alternative. He claimed that either the prisoner had been driven insane by his early sufferings and his wife's behaviour, or alternatively that he had sufficiently lost control of himself to justify a jury in returning a verdict of manslaughter. In putting forward the defence of insanity he did not allege that the prisoner had imagined he was really an elephant, but simply that his mind had become unhinged. It was proved that George was a quiet little man who had never offered violence to anyone. Relations and friends testified that his conduct towards his wife was unexceptionable.

"Why," said Sir Gordon, "should this meek and mild little man kill his wife if he were not either insane or goaded beyond human endurance? I listened to your names, members of the jury, as they were read out. You will not think it offensive of me if I say that they were all ordinary names. How happy you must be that they are. I do not, however, ask you to acquit the prisoner of murder from motives of thankfulness or pity. I ask you to listen to the evidence of eminent doctors. They will tell you that the mind of the accused man has been affected from his earliest childhood by his extraordinary name. They have elicited from him under psychoanalysis that his nurses and governesses used to enrage him by making fun of it. At the time, he was probably unaware of the fact, but it set up in his mind a germ which was fed and nurtured by the boys at school, by his business acquaintances, by practical jokers, and finally by his unfortunate wife. These doctors are prepared to state that, in their opinion, the mind of the accused may well have been in such a state that he was not, at the time he killed his wife, fully responsible for his actions."

Sir Gordon said much more in the same strain and, when he felt that he had sufficiently impressed the Judge and the jury, he called his witnesses. The general effect of the medical evidence on both sides was that the accused was not insane but that he was sensitive to an abnormal degree to jests made about his name.

No doctor would say the accused would have killed his wife if a policeman had been in the room at the time, nor would any of them say that he did not realise that it was wrong to kill your wife, even if she did call you Jumbo and offer you a bun.

The doctors for the defence, however, were emphatic in stating that the accused might have been goaded into such a fury – the culminating result of pent-up suffering – that he was deprived of ordinary self-control. The doctors for the prosecution were much less emphatic on this point, but agreed that it was possible.

After a careful trial and summing up by the Judge, George was found not guilty of murder, but guilty of manslaughter, and sentenced to seven years' penal servitude. That, however, was not the end of the matter, as the case had by this time aroused considerable interest. There did not come into existence a league for the protection of persons with awkward names, but a Bill was presented to Parliament to make it a serious offence to use the telephone for such purposes as have been mentioned. Moreover, numerous letters were written to the newspapers both by the possessors of unusual names and by those who sympathised with them. Learned articles were written by psychiatrists, and the case of George Elephant attained considerably more notoriety than the facts, as they appeared in the first instance, seemed to warrant. In the end, so much sympathy was shown for George and so much pressure put on the Government that the Home Secretary was persuaded to advise His Majesty to reduce the sentence to one of three years' penal servitude. This meant that George would be released after a little more than two years, provided that he earned full good conduct marks.

The Home Secretary had been urged to order his immediate release, but he had stood firm and said that George must be taught a sufficient lesson before he was let out. He also reminded the House that, if any lighter sentence were ordered, the lives of unwanted husbands or wives whose names ended in "bottom" might be in considerable jeopardy.

Two years later, just before his release, a new and slightly pompous chaplain arrived at the prison where George was serving his sentence.

He had a chat with George. "It may be," he said, "that you have been more sinned against than sinning, but, before you leave, would you like to say anything to me in confidence so that you may feel that, when you quit these walls, you are starting really afresh – with your soul cleansed of your sin?"

George hesitated.

"You can trust me, you know," went on the chaplain, "and I feel that there might be something – even something quite small – of which you would like to unburden yourself. Perhaps I can help you. Start telling me in your own words the story of your crime – for, whatever excuse there may have been for it, a crime it was. Tell me, for instance, what was it that actually led you to kill your wife?"

"Well, as a matter of fact," said George, "I was fond of another woman."

CHAPTER SIX

The Case Of Mr Tinker

There was complete silence when the Professor ceased talking. He had thought it a good little story and expected at least an appreciative chuckle. Eventually one of the audience broke the silence.

"Go on, Professor," he said, "finish it."

"I'm afraid I have," said the Professor. Then, feeling that something was required of him, he added, "I expect he came out of prison and lived happily ever after."

"Why didn't you say so before?"

"I'd forgotten."

"Are you quite sure he lived happily ever after?"

"Yes – quite sure."

"Well, that's all right then," said another man.

"I must say I like a story with a point," said Mr Wilkins.

"I quite agree," began the Professor. "Then why don't you tell one?"

"Yes, a story with a point," said one or two others together, "a story with a point."

The Professor began to wonder whether they would rise and tear him limb from limb. At that moment one of the nurses came in. "Now, what's going on in here?" she asked.

"We want a story with a point," said a patient.

"Yes, that's what we want," said another.

"What's all this business about stories?" said the nurse.

"I'm afraid I've just told a story," said the Professor.

"Well, you shouldn't," said the nurse. "It makes you excited and everyone else too. You'd better go to bed."

"But Dr Long asked me to," complained the Professor.

"Now, don't argue," said the nurse. "You've come here to rest, not to tell stories. Now, off to bed with you." The Professor was very angry, but he did not show it. Without a word he got up and went to his room.

In the morning he asked to see Dr Long. "I'm afraid you'll have to wait until after lunch," said the Sister. "He will be engaged all the morning."

"But it's important," said the Professor.

"So's his engagement," said the Sister. "Now – run along."

Again the Professor retained his control, comforting himself with the thought that he would not be treated like a small boy much longer. He waited impatiently for his interview. As far as possible, he avoided the other patients, but Mr Wilkins came up to him while he was strolling in the garden. He gave the Professor one of his swift, sidelong glances and then said, "You remember what I told you last night?" The Professor did not, but to save argument he said that he did. "Well, keep it to yourself."

"I will," said the Professor.

"By the way," said Mr Wilkins, "what was it?"

The Professor thought quickly. "I'd better not tell you here, someone might hear us."

"Well, why not?" said Mr Wilkins. "There's no secret about it."

"Excuse me," said the Professor, "I must go," and he made off quickly for another part of the garden. Mr

Wilkins scratched his head. "Poor fellow," he said. "Quite mad." Then glancing furtively all round him, as if to make sure he was alone, he sat down in a deck chair.

The Professor managed to keep out of everyone's way until lunchtime. Then he came in, had his lunch, and went at once to Dr Long's room. "What do you want?" said the Sister.

"I want to see Dr Long."

"Tomorrow morning," said the Sister.

"But you told me he'd be free after lunch."

"Tomorrow morning," repeated the Sister.

"Now – look here," began the Professor, but he got no further before the Sister interrupted. "If I have any more nonsense from you, you'll go into 'A' Ward. Now run off." The Professor did not know what was meant by "A" Ward, but there was an ominous sound about it which made him check the words he was longing to utter. "Oh, well," he thought to himself, "I can just about stand another twenty-four hours – but not a minute longer." Somehow or other he whiled away the time between meals. Immediately after dinner he went to his room. He was on the point of undressing when there was a knock at the door and one of the patients walked in. "I'm just going to bed," said the Professor.

"That's all right," said the patient, "I don't mind."

"But I do," said the Professor.

"You aren't turning nasty, are you?" asked the patient, with a glint in his eye the Professor did not quite like. He looked for the bell. Then the thought of "A" ward struck him. If he rang, a nurse would come. She might think that he was the one in the wrong. "Of course not," he said. "What can I do for you?"

"A story please, Professor, and make it one with a point."

"By all means," said the Professor. "Won't you sit down?"

"You don't catch me that way. You sit down and I'll stand up."

"You may get rather tired," said the Professor. "I can't think of a very short one."

"Never mind. When I'm tired of one leg I'll stand on the other. Now are you going to begin at the beginning or in the middle?"

"Whichever you prefer," said the Professor.

"It doesn't matter," said the patient. "I can always hear the part I missed the second time through."

"I'll begin at the beginning, I think," said the Professor. "Are you ready?"

"Shoot," said the patient.

"I should like to," thought the Professor, but, instead, he told him "The Case of Mr Tinker."

The Case Of Mr Tinker

"Accordingly the action fails and must be dismissed with costs." With these words Mr Justice Hawley disposed of the now famous Tinker invention case. Oswald Tinker, who had invented what he had claimed to be an entirely new type of weapon, could hardly believe that it was true. He had worked for years at his invention and had been advised by eminent counsel that his claim was a good one. Now the case was over and he had lost. His life's work had been wasted.

He walked slowly away from the courts along the Strand towards Waterloo Bridge. He had made up his mind as to the only course now open to him. He had vaguely heard the various statements made by his counsel and solicitors after the case ... "the Judge is wrong" ... "appeal" ...

"certain to succeed" … but they had meant nothing to him. He reached the bridge, climbed on the parapet and, before anyone could stop him, he had jumped into the Thames. However, a police boat happened to be near at the time and he was rescued wet and unhappy.

In due course he appeared at Bow Street police court before Mr Grantley. The facts were stated by the policeman who had fished him out of the water, and Mr Grantley asked Mr Tinker if he had anything to say about the matter.

"I wanted a swim," said Mr Tinker.

"Remanded for medical report," said Mr Grantley.

A week later Mr Tinker appeared in the dock again. Mr Grantley addressed him: "This report says that you are quite sane but that you are depressed as a result of losing a patent action," he said.

"Very depressed," said Mr Tinker. "Wouldn't you be?"

"Very likely," said Mr Grantley, "but it's cowardly to give way. Besides," he added, "if you have been advised by such well-known experts that your claim is a good one, why don't you appeal? I know nothing of the case, but the Judge may have been wrong. They are sometimes, you know. Everyone makes mistakes. I can't pretend that I'm always right. I was wrong about you, for instance. I thought you were just mad. I was misled by your saying that you wanted a swim. By the way, why did you say that?"

"Did I say that?" said Mr Tinker. "How very stupid of me. I don't like swimming at all. Perhaps you misunderstood me. Perhaps my moustache got in the way."

"Well, never mind about that now," said Mr Grantley. "But why don't you think about appealing?"

"The costs," sighed Mr Tinker. "Such a very expensive matter. Every time Sir Walter opens his mouth it costs me a guinea. And he keeps on opening it. Do you know it costs me five guineas to go and see him even? Of course, I could see him for nothing if I just waited outside the courts and watched him go in and out, but then I shouldn't get any advice. I suppose you couldn't lend me a half a crown," he added hopefully.

"Now don't be foolish," said Mr Grantley. "If I let you go, will you see the Poor Persons Department? They might be able to help you."

"I'll see anybody," said Mr Tinker, "but I'm not very hopeful if I don't have Sir Walter. After all, it was he who advised me that I was right. Perhaps the Judge was a pacifist and was prejudiced. Would that be likely?"

"Now don't ask silly questions. If I bind you over to be of good behaviour will you promise not to do it again?"

"Oh, certainly," said Mr Tinker. "It was most unpleasant. I should use a gas oven next time."

"That's quite enough," said Mr Grantley. "Either you'll give me your promise not to attempt suicide again or you'll go to prison. Which is it to be?"

"The costs are so heavy," said Mr Tinker. "Do you think Sir Walter would conduct the appeal for nothing?"

"Mr Tinker," almost shouted the magistrate. "I've a lot of other cases to try. Will you give me your promise or not?"

"Oh, I'll promise," said Mr Tinker – "but the costs are really awful," he added.

Mr Grantley duly bound over Mr Tinker and he left the dock. After he had gone out of the court room he went up to one of the policemen who had been in court. "What did I promise?" he asked.

"Not to do it again," said the policeman.

"Oh! Was that all?" said Mr Tinker, and, leaving the court, he started off for Waterloo Bridge.

He had not gone very far when he was caught up by one of the reporters who had been in court.

"Good morning, Mr Tinker," said the reporter.

"Oh, it's you," said Mr Tinker. "Have I met you before?"

"I don't think so – but I just heard your case in court. May I have a word with you? I think I may be able to help."

"Oh – I can get up on the parapet quite easily by myself, thank you," said Mr Tinker.

"No, I don't mean that," said the reporter. "I may be able to help about the costs."

"Oh, how nice," said Mr Tinker. "Will you pay them?"

"Not quite that," said the reporter, "but my newspaper might help you to do so. How about it?"

"Oh, very nice indeed," said Mr Tinker. "That is exactly what I should like."

"Good. Now come with me to my office and we'll see what can be done."

They went to the offices of the *Daily Sun* and the upshot of it was that an appeal was made to the public on behalf of Mr Tinker. There was little news at the time and the reporter had rightly seen an opening. Poor little Mr Tinker, with his moustache and his umbrella and his beautiful invention. Sir Walter had undoubtedly advised that the patent was valid, and it was a shame that the big armament manufacturers should have defeated this hard-working little man.

The money was obtained and the appeal duly launched. It came on for hearing some three months later. The last words of the Master of the Rolls' judgment had a familiar ring in Mr Tinker's ears. They were – "Accordingly this appeal fails and will be dismissed with costs."

Once again Mr Tinker left the Strand for Waterloo Bridge. Once again he climbed on to the parapet – but this time, just as he was about to jump, he was seized by an observant and energetic young man and handed over to a policeman. In due course he appeared before Mr Grantley at Bow Street. The facts were recited.

"Well?" said Mr Grantley.

"Another swim," said Mr Tinker.

"I'm not going to stand this nonsense," said Mr Grantley. "You just won't try. Everything possible has been done for you and all you do is to pretend that you're simple-minded in order to excite sympathy. You've had your appeal conducted for nothing. I'm very sorry that it's failed, but it's just one of those things."

"One of which things?" said Mr Tinker.

"I'm not going to take any notice of your impertinence," replied the magistrate. "There's only one thing to do with you."

"I should like to appeal to the House of Lords," said Mr Tinker, "but it's the costs. So very heavy. Could you lend me five shillings, d'you think?"

"You'll go to prison for three months," said Mr Grantley. "And you must learn that it is only a coward who gives in."

"I would prefer to go to the House of Lords," said Mr Tinker.

"Call the next case," said the magistrate.

So Mr Tinker was led away and he spent the next three months in Wormwood Scrubs. But the *Daily Sun* was still short of material, and Mr Tinker had, in quite a short time, become a sort of symbol of the little man who was being bludgeoned by the magnate. His imprisonment almost made him a martyr. More funds were raised and notice of appeal to the House of Lords was given, leave to appeal having already been obtained. The appeal came on for hearing some time after Mr Tinker's release. He had served his full three months. Being unused to discipline, he had not taken kindly to the prison rules and, although the Governor and warders had done everything they could to help him, he was unable to earn any good conduct marks at all. It was really quite pitiful to see hardened prison warders striving for all they were worth to persuade Mr Tinker to be amenable to prison routine. They almost went on their knees and begged him to behave. The efforts which the Governor made to find some grounds for giving him just a few conduct marks were most praiseworthy. But Mr Tinker was adamant.

"It is perfectly reasonable to swim," he said, "and I will walk and talk just as I wish. Besides," he would add, "the costs are very heavy indeed."

Of course, at first he was seen by a psychiatrist, but he reported that Mr Tinker was entirely sane and had merely come to the conclusion that a pretence of simple-mindedness would help him. He certainly had an obstinacy complex, but that was all. During his sentence he had heard that an appeal was being made on his behalf, but although he agreed to it, he did not seem very interested.

"It will be the same again," he said, "but at any rate Sir Walter will be pleased."

The appeal in the House of Lords lasted for a week, and it was not until a further three weeks after the argument that judgment was delivered by the presiding Law Lord. Mr Tinker listened with considerable interest to the technical passages in the judgment, but he had made up his mind that the ending would be the same as in the previous courts. To his surprise, however, Lord Stone ended his judgment with the following words: "I accordingly move, your Lordships, that this appeal be allowed with costs, to include the costs of the hearings in the Court of Appeal and before Mr Justice Hawley."

Four other similar judgments were delivered and Mr Tinker left the House of Lords in a state of great elation. This time, instead of making for Waterloo Bridge, he went straight to Bow Street police court and requested a private interview with Mr Grantley. The magistrate hesitated, but, having heard from a reporter that the Tinker case had been won, he decided to see him in his private room.

"I have only come here to thank you," said Mr Tinker. "I cannot tell you how grateful I am. It is entirely through you that I have won my case."

"I'm delighted at the result," said the magistrate. "It only shows how stupid it is to despair, doesn't it?"

"It does indeed," said Mr Tinker. "I don't mind telling you that I was extremely angry at being sentenced by you – but if you hadn't sent me to prison, I'm sure no one would have paid those dreadful costs. So thank you very much indeed."

And Mr Tinker got up to go. The magistrate shook hands with him and he started for the door. Then he turned round.

"Would it interest you to see the invention? I have an exact model on me."

"Very much," said Mr Grantley.

Mr Tinker fished in his pockets and brought out the model.

"As you have read, the actual weapon, which is fifty times this size, fires a projectile weighing 200 lbs and makes practically no sound. This little model fires a revolver bullet and makes no sound at all."

And, turning again for the door, he left Mr Grantley collapsed in a chair with a bullet in his heart.

CHAPTER SEVEN

Not On The Menu

"Now that's what I call a story with a point," said the patient when the Professor had finished. "I liked that."

"I'm so glad," said the Professor. "Now do you think I might go to bed?"

"Why, of course. I hope I haven't been keeping you up."

"Not at all," said the Professor. "Only too pleased."

"Well – I'll say good night then," said the patient, and started to go. At the door he paused and said, "Oh – by the way, why did Mr Tinker kill him?"

"Because he was mad," said the Professor – and then felt a little uncomfortable.

"Who was mad? The magistrate?"

"No, Mr Tinker."

"He seemed sane enough to me. Did they hang him?"

"I don't know. I should doubt it."

"But I thought that was the point?"

"Quite," said the Professor, who, though completely out of his depth, thought that agreement was the wisest policy.

"Perhaps it was only a dream, after all," went on the patient. "Have you thought of that as an idea for a short story? At the end you just put 'it was only a dream.' It's most effective."

"I will try it some time," said the Professor.

"Don't do it too often or people will know it's coming."

"I'll be careful of that," said the Professor.

"Well, good night and thank you," said the patient, "but if I were you, I should make a slight alteration in the story."

"Oh – yes?" said the Professor.

"I should make the magistrate shoot Mr Tinker instead."

"An excellent idea," said the Professor – and he meant it. To his relief the patient left him, and at last he was able to undress and go to bed.

He slept surprisingly well, and after breakfast he went straight to Dr Long's room.

"Oh, you're here again," said the Sister. "You'll have to wait."

"Very well," said the Professor.

"It's no good waiting here," said the Sister. " Go and sit in the lounge and amuse yourself. I'll send for you when the doctor's ready."

The Professor went to the lounge, picked up a magazine and tried to read, but he found it very difficult. After an hour and a half he got up and walked towards Dr Long's room. The Sister came out at the same moment and made an impatient gesture, waving him back to the lounge. By this time the Professor's nerves were becoming a little frayed, and he would cheerfully have throttled the Sister.

"I mustn't think of things like that," he said to himself, "or I'll become like everyone else here."

"Good morning," said a jovial-looking middle-aged man, who had just sat down beside him. "I don't think we've met before."

"Good morning," said the Professor. "I don't think we have."

"Well, it's never too late to mend," said the jovial-looking man, whose name was Abbot. "You're the sort of man I've been looking for."

"Oh, yes?" said the Professor.

"Yes. I believe I could sell you something."

"I'm afraid," began the Professor, but Mr Abbot interrupted.

"Oh – not really of course. Just in fun. It's a very good game. Now I have five thousand penknives to offer you. At the moment they're in Nicaragua. I can let you have them at £3 per gross f.o.b. Nicaragua or £3 2s 6d ex warehouse Liverpool. What do you say?"

The Professor was not commercially minded, although he had some vague recollections of a few commercial cases he had done in his early days at the Bar.

"I don't really want any penknives," he said. "I could do with one though," he added.

"I couldn't sell as little as a gross."

"I didn't mean a gross. I meant one penknife."

"Oh – you're hopeless," said Mr Abbot. "We'll try again. Now I have a fleet of second-hand Daimler cars. Fifty of them. All in first-class condition. None of them more than three years old. What will you offer – delivered anywhere you like in England or Wales?"

"I suppose I may have them examined first?" said the Professor.

"That's much better," said Mr Abbot. "Now you're really coming on. Yes – certainly. I have our engineer's reports

74

here which your own engineers can check. How much will you offer subject to inspection?"

"I'm afraid I'll have to consult my partner," said the Professor. "I can't quote a price without his sanction."

"Better and better," said Mr Abbot. "This is real fun. Aren't you enjoying it?"

"Tremendously," said the Professor, looking hopefully towards the door for the Sister to come for him. She did not come, however, and two hours later, when the Professor had bought and sold every conceivable kind of commodity on terms which varied from cash down to a series of bills payable every three months, the maid announced lunch. Again the Professor was alone within ten seconds of the announcement. As he went out of the room he saw the Sister.

"Oh, there you are," she said. "I've been looking all over the place for you. Well – it's too late now. You'll have to come the day after tomorrow."

"What about tomorrow?"

"Tomorrow is Sunday," said the Sister. "The doctor must have some rest. Now go and have your lunch."

Somehow or other the Professor managed to get through that day and the next, and on the day after that he actually secured his interview with Dr Long.

"Yes, Professor, what can I do for you?" said Dr Long.

"I'm afraid I shall have to leave," said the Professor. "Please don't take any offence, but I'm just not happy here. I think I'll go up to Scotland and do a little fishing."

"But I'm afraid that's quite impossible," said the doctor.

"It is not only not impossible," said the Professor, who had had enough by this time, "but I shall leave this afternoon. I will pay my bill at once, and shall be obliged if you will arrange for a car to take me to the station."

"I think there's a little misunderstanding," said the doctor. "You can't leave here – unless, of course, you choose to go to a public institution. I don't imagine you would care for that."

"What on earth do you mean?" said the Professor. "There's nothing wrong with me except the little bother of which you know. You speak as though I were a certified lunatic."

"You are, Professor," said the doctor. "Now – don't get excited or upset. Everything is going to be quite all right." The Professor had gone very pale and looked as though he might faint.

"Sit down for a moment. I'll get you a drink." The Professor sat down. After he had had some whisky, the colour started to come back to his cheeks.

"Good God," he said. "It can't be; what is supposed to be wrong with me?"

"Now – don't worry about that," said the doctor. "I'm quite sure you'll be absolutely all right in a few weeks."

"I feel absolutely all right now," said the Professor. "I've never felt better. It's just that extraordinary sensation I get when I start to lecture."

"I know," said the doctor, "but I'm sure we'll find the answer to that and get you quite normal again."

"Are all the people here certified?" asked the Professor.

"Oh, yes," said the doctor.

"That accounts for everything. I didn't realise it before. Perhaps I should have. But, seriously, you don't look on me as you do on the others, do you?"

"Professor, every affection of the mind is different. You can find dangerous homicidal maniacs – no, don't look alarmed, we don't have any here – who are perfectly rational and behave like ordinary sane men, except when they come up against one particular circumstance. Then they act like raving lunatics. It may only happen once in six months. It may not happen at all if the circumstance does not arise, but as long as there is the possibility that the circumstance will arise and that they will react to it in the way I have mentioned, it is essential for public safety that they should be under permanent control. In your case, you are, as you say, a perfectly normal, sane man in every way – except when you come up against the one particular circumstance which affects you. Then you behave, as you know, quite irrationally, as no sane man would behave. I wouldn't tell you all this if I were not quite satisfied that your form of insanity is a mild one and that we shall cure you in a very short time. But, if you ask me if I look on you as I do upon the other patients, I am bound to say that I do. Each of them has his own particular kink. With some it is obvious for twenty-three hours out of twenty-four."

"I should say it is," interrupted the Professor.

"With others," went on the doctor, "like yourself, it is not noticeable until the particular circumstance arises. Now – I know it is easy for me to say 'don't worry', but I can assure you that your time will pass much more quickly, and will in fact be much shorter, if you can make yourself refrain from worrying."

"How long am I likely to be here?" asked the Professor.

"Obviously I can't give you a definite answer to that question, but at a very rough estimate I would say not more than six months."

"Six months!" said the Professor with dismay in his voice.

"Possibly much less," soothed the doctor; "it all depends. Now you're looking much better. Is there anything else you'd like to ask?"

"Nothing at all, thank you," said the Professor. "I'm very much obliged to you and I'm sorry if I've been a nuisance."

"You haven't at all. I'm glad to have helped. Come and see me whenever you want. Just speak to the Sister first."

The Professor went out. He went straight to his room and sat down. He had fully made up his mind what to do. The only question was how and when to do it. Sane or insane he was not going to remain at Tapworth House.

While the Professor was working out his plans for escape the Master of St James' was reading the story submitted to him by Mr Pringle.

Here it is.

Not On The Menu

I like to see happy united families, but, except for that, it is no concern of mine whether you deceive your wife. Before you start on your downward path, however, be warned by the fate of George Harkaway, and consider the end to which it may lead you. George joined the ranks of the married after 1923, but he seemed to think that he had joined at pre-1923 rates. For the benefit of those who think that this expression has relation to the Royal Warrant for the Pay of the Army, let me explain that before 1923 a husband was – by law, at any rate – pretty well licensed to be unfaithful to his wife, provided he did not beat or desert her as well. George would never have thought of beating or leaving his wife. He was a very nice fellow in many respects, but he was too much inclined to succumb to the temptations of a charming face or an attractive figure. While he assumed that his wife behaved herself perfectly, as she was before and since 1923 bound by law to do, he never even tried to behave himself – certainly not after the first two years of his marriage. He was devoted to his wife and would have been quite heartbroken had she divorced him, but, finding that it was apparently quite easy to deceive her, he did so constantly. Indeed, until the events of which I am about to tell you, he both had his cake and ate it, and found it very pleasant.

One spring morning George got up, full of the joy of living. His hot bath seemed even better than usual, the crisp morning air which greeted him as he stepped on the balcony for his morning sniff before breakfast gave him a pleasant tingling sensation, and Margaret, his wife, looked younger and brighter than ever as she came into the dining-room. Funnily enough when George had sinned, or was about to sin, so far from looking for blemishes in his wife he did just the opposite. It was so comforting to think: I am just going with Betty or Millicent or April to have a gorgeous time – and nevertheless I have at home here as lovely a woman as any of them – a woman more intelligent than most of them – a woman who really understands me and whose main object in life is to make me happy. She knows all the little comforts I like – my sherry and salted almonds before dinner – my slippers just warmed – the exact way my eggs and bacon should be cooked – the soups I like – the temperature of my bath – the shirts I prefer – everything in fact which goes to make me a happy man. So thought George that spring morning.

"You look charming, darling," he said.

"Compliments before breakfast, George?" she answered. "It sounds as though you're going to be late at the office tonight."

"How did you guess?"

"Oh – when one's been married to you for ten years one does guess somehow, darling."

"Clever girl."

"Aren't I?"

Was there a gleam of something he had not previously noticed in Margaret's eyes as she said "Aren't I?"

"Well, let's have some breakfast," he said.

"It's just coming, darling."

They sat down and each picked up a paper. They had the same ideas about breakfast. Bacon and eggs – they were essential – coffee and a paper. Occasionally they had tea instead of coffee and talked instead of reading, but bacon and eggs neither of them ever changed. The maid came in. She brought the coffee and put it in front of Margaret. She went out again and came in with a plate of bacon and eggs, which she gave to Margaret. Margaret poured out the coffee and gave George a cup.

"Thank you, darling," he said, and returned to the paper. Margaret began to eat. George read for a time and then the inner George called him up and said, "What about me? I'm empty and it's too dark to read down here."

"Breakfast coming soon, darling?" he asked. Curious he should have to say that. Nothing was ever late. Margaret saw to that.

"It's here, darling," said Margaret, still reading the paper. He looked up. He could see nothing except Margaret eating her eggs and bacon. That was funny too, because he was always served first.

"No, it's not, darling," he said.

"Oh, yes it is," said Margaret. "Look, it's lovely and I'm enjoying it," and she held up a piece of crisp bacon with a suspicion of mustard on it.

"But where's mine?" he said.

"Yours? Oh – yours – darling – oh – of course, your eggs and bacon – that's what you mean, darling?"

"Yes, of course that's what I mean. What d'you think I mean?"

He was starting to get irritated – a most unusual occurrence. Nothing ever happened to irritate him – not at home at any rate.

"I'm afraid there isn't any for you this morning, darling," she said. "But just you watch me enjoying mine."

"What on earth's the matter? Why have they run out? It's ridiculous."

"Oh, they haven't run out, darling. I just said you wouldn't want any this morning."

"You said I wouldn't want any this morning? Whatever for? Of course I want some. I never said anything about not wanting any. Have you gone mad all of a sudden – or what?"

"Do you really want to know, George darling?"

"Of course I want to know. Why shouldn't I have my breakfast?"

"I'll tell you, my sweet – when I've finished. Now, don't ring the bell, because we don't want a scene before Judy, and if she comes I shall tell her you don't want any breakfast and you will tell her you do, and it will be so muddling for her and she might give notice. So just sit quiet and enjoy your coffee and toast until I've finished – there's a good boy."

I have said that George would never have thought of beating his wife, and when I add that the thought never occurred to him even on this occasion you will agree that he had some good points.

He got up and went to the balcony while Margaret went on serenely – or with apparent serenity – eating her breakfast. She was, in fact, excited and hardly noticed what she was eating. The great moment was at hand. What would be the result? Outwardly she remained completely calm.

"Now, George," she called, "I'm ready." He came in. "Sit down and listen to me." Margaret had never spoken to him as if he were a small boy before, but he obeyed.

"Well," he said, in an effort to grow up all of a sudden. "What is this all about?"

"It's about you, darling, and about Fifi and Melanie and Topsy – or whatever their names are. Is there one called Fifi, darling?"

"No," he said sulkily.

"I'm so glad, darling. I don't mind the other two."

"Well, there isn't a Melanie or a Topsy either."

"How many are there, George?"

"What has that got to do with my breakfast?"

"Everything, George. You see, I've decided to do something about it, and, without going into unnecessary details, this is what I've decided. I don't think you want to leave me, but I'm not prepared to go on sharing you with so many. I felt that, if you knew that I knew all about it, it might make a difference."

"I dare say, but what's this got to do with my breakfast?"

"I'm telling you, darling. I think it would be so unpleasant for me to say to you in the morning 'Who were you out with last night?', or when you come back at night 'Have you been with Matilda?' Don't you agree, darling? It would be horrid. I couldn't do it. So very ugly, too. It would quite spoil the home. So, instead, I've hit on an idea. Every time I think you've been out with a girl friend I shall deprive you of one of your home comforts. Then you'll know that I know, darling. Don't you think it's a good notion? So much more pleasant than question and answer. No wrangling – no cross-examination – just no breakfast or no slippers – or no sherry – d'you follow, darling? And, of course, it will make it just a weeny bit more uncomfortable for you, darling – just to help you remember for the next time. Then you can say to yourself – Now let me see, is Caroline worth more than bacon and eggs? Shall it be Matilda or salted almonds? Don't tell them of course, darling, they'd be terribly hurt."

"Why haven't you told me before?"

"Why haven't *you*, darling? But don't let's start these silly questionings. That's just what I want to avoid. Now finish your coffee and go off to work. If you don't find your bed made when you come home you'll know you have been out with Ermintrude."

"I wish you wouldn't choose these ridiculous names."

"I wish you wouldn't choose the people, darling."

There was a short silence. He finished his coffee and got up to go. He had been going to say that he'd be late back from the office, but he couldn't now.

"Well – goodbye, darling. See you this evening," he said, and kissed her.

"Darling," she said, "do have a good lunch."

He left for the office in a very troubled frame of mind. Of one thing he was quite certain. He did not want to lose Margaret. Undoubtedly, though, however lightly she had put it, there was a grim warning in what she said. He felt sure of that. It was a shame, and the fact that it was nobody's fault but his own did not help in the least. It would have been an advantage if he could have felt that Margaret was unfair to him. But she hadn't been in the least unfair and he knew it. No, he must not lose her. At the same time he did not want to give up his various sideshows – least of all Anne. He was really fond of Anne

– not, of course, in the way in which he was fond of Margaret, but sufficiently to make him jealous if he knew she was going out alone with another man. He was due to take her out himself that evening. What about it? He picked up the telephone as soon as he reached the office.

"Hometown 1783. Hullo – is that Anne?"

"Yes, of course, darling."

"Anne – I'm terribly sorry but – now look here – you must let me finish – yes, it is about tonight – I'm terribly, terribly sorry – how did you know? – no, it's really quite impossible – no really it isn't – you know I wouldn't put you off for anyone – I'll explain another time – do be reasonable, darling – all right, go out with Dick Bayley – no, darling, I didn't mean that – I – hullo – hullo – Oh, damn!" and he hung up the receiver.

"Damn!" he said again as his secretary came in.

"Anything the matter?" she asked. She was everything, or nearly everything, you could expect the secretary of a man like George Harkaway to be.

"Yes – everything," he answered.

"I'm so sorry," she said sympathetically, and came over to him and squeezed his hand. It helped him quite a lot. Isabel Carstairs was the most understanding girl. She knew that she was only one of many, but she never let it make the slightest difference. She was always ready to help when she was wanted. She never intruded when she was not wanted.

"You're a darling," he said, "where shall we have lunch?"

In due course they went to Boulestin and he told her how miserable he was. She was more understanding than ever. They had an excellent lunch and drank more than usual. They did not get back to the office until late, and on the way they decided that after work he must take her back to her flat for a drink before he went home. They gave effect to this decision, and he had rather more than a drink. He reached home in time for dinner.

"Good evening, darling," he said. "You see – I'm not late."

"Sweet of you, darling," she said.

The shoes were there, the sherry, the salted almonds – everything just as he liked it.

"You're a darling," he said – but when he went to bed he found that it had not been made.

As he got up the next morning, he began to wonder how much more he would have to pay for his attentions to Isabel on the previous day. Would there be bacon and eggs? Toast? Coffee? Perhaps there would be no breakfast at all. Or was the unmade bed to be taken as a sufficient reminder? He found that it was. Breakfast was just as usual with everything he wanted. After breakfast he went over to his wife.

"I'll try to be good," he said as he kissed her goodbye.

"I'm sure you will, darling," she said.

For some weeks afterwards things went very well. Occasionally he found no sherry or no slippers – but then he couldn't drop Anne just like that. He did, however, by great strength of mind eventually manage to reconcile himself to the idea of life without Anne at all. She was most unpleasant about it – which made things easier.

Isabel helped him to get rid of the others by talking to them on the phone and lying so blatantly that eventually they ceased to ring him up. Isabel herself still remained – but she never nagged him or complained that he did not take her out. Occasionally he had to weigh up in his mind whether kissing Isabel was worth no salted almonds. How Margaret guessed so accurately he could not fathom – until one day when he came home, radiant in his blamelessness, to find no slippers warming by the fire. "Have I made a mistake, darling?" she exclaimed, when she saw by his face of genuine innocence that she had.

"I'm so sorry." It happened again from time to time, and, as he was now almost entirely virtuous, he became annoyed. On the strength of his annoyance he took Isabel out one day. Returning home with a guilty conscience he found everything in order. The mistake was in his favour this time.

And so it went on – and quite satisfactorily on the whole. The penalties exacted from him by Margaret became less and less frequent while his affair with Isabel was progressing most pleasantly. It wasn't at all a bad existence, he thought. After all – while there is safety in numbers, two are much easier to deal with than twenty – particularly when one of the two is the sympathetic Isabel and the other is a really lovely wife. So all went well until one day, when they were at breakfast and he was enjoying his full quota of bacon and eggs, he happened to look up and saw that his wife was eating toast.

"Aren't you hungry, darling?" he said. "Why no bacon and eggs?"

"Oh, George," she said, and looked out of the window.

CHAPTER EIGHT

The Dream

When he had finished the Master sent for Mr Pringle.

"Is this your own unaided work?" he asked.

"I had some help with it," admitted Mr Pringle.

"Who helped you?"

"As a matter of fact, Master, it was a Newnham girl."

"Well, the result isn't bad at all. I should send it to the *Granta*."

"Thank you, sir."

"At the same time I should advise you not to mix up your legal studies with your literary career."

"I'll see it doesn't happen again, Master."

"Very well, then. Now you'd better find your accomplice and tell her the result of your efforts."

"As a matter of fact she's coming to tea, Master."

"Then I won't keep you any more. Good afternoon, Pringle."

"Good afternoon, Master."

Mr Pringle reached his rooms just as Mary arrived. After they had started tea, he said, "The Master liked that story."

"I should hope so," said Mary.

"Why are you so sure about it?"

"My uncle gets paid twenty pounds for a story like

that."

"But he didn't write it – did he?"

"Of course, he did, silly. Give me another meringue."

"How did you get hold of it?"

"In an old magazine."

"But you swore it wasn't out of a magazine."

I know, idiot; if I hadn't, you wouldn't have used it."

"You're completely unprincipled, Mary," he said.

"That depends on what you mean by principle," said Mary. "I have my own code."

"But you told me a deliberate lie."

"Of course, I did. Have you never told one? People make too much fuss about lies. It isn't the lie that matters, it's the object of the lie."

"I've never looked at it that way," said Mr Pringle. "Well, have a try," said Mary, "but give me another meringue first. Even the most truthful people tell a certain number of lies. They call them social lies or white lies. But they are lies just the same. 'Would you like to come to tea?' 'I should love it.' Just a lie. No, I wasn't referring to today. I really love having tea with you, and I should have said 'No' if I hadn't wanted to come. Now, if you adopt my principles, those lies become quite innocuous, and at time same time you are not put in the impossible position of having to pretend they're not really lies. My rule is a simple one. Lie as much as you like, but never tell a lie with a mean object. I lied to help you. That isn't a mean object, is it, George?" And she looked him full in the face. She had lovely eyes and she knew it. So did he.

"When you look at me like that," he said, "I couldn't disagree with you about anything. I think you are adorable."

"More, please," said Mary, and there was more.

Meanwhile, the Professor had decided on his plan of

action. He had made up his mind to leave all his belongings at the home. It would be too difficult to escape with even one suitcase. He had a little money with him and he would go straight to an old friend of his in London. There he could obtain sufficient funds. He could buy some more clothes and travel round the country until his certification became out of date. He knew that, if a lunatic remained at large for fourteen days, he must be recertified. He was quite determined on remaining at large for the necessary period and not being recertified. He strolled casually out of his bedroom towards the door leading to the garden. On the way he met the Sister.

"Oh, Sister," he said, "I'm going into the garden. D'you think I'd be wise to wear a hat?" She was quite used to similar inquiries.

"Yes, I should," she said, "if you find it too hot without one."

"Thank you, Sister," said the Professor. "I'll go and get it." He walked back to his bedroom, collected his hat and wandered into the garden. He went as far as possible away from the house, and, making certain that no one was in view, he managed to squeeze himself through a hedge. He found himself in a small lane, rather dishevelled but free. It was quite an exciting adventure. He brushed himself down and, when he was satisfied that he was sufficiently presentable, started down the lane. He was some miles from the station, but he hoped to get a lift. He was lucky, and within half an hour he had caught a train to London. The train was not a corridor train, and he was in a compartment with a woman of forty or so and her daughter of about seventeen. After they had been travelling for an hour they stopped in a tunnel. They had been stationary a few minutes when he noticed that the woman was fidgeting.

"D'you think we'll be long here?" she said.

"I shouldn't think so," said the Professor.

"I hope not. I don't like it," said the woman.

"Don't worry, Mother," said the daughter. "We'll soon be off again." They were still there five minutes later.

"I wonder if anything is the matter," said the woman.

"Nothing at all," said the Professor, who realised that the woman suffered from claustrophobia. "I wonder if you'd mind my telling you a story. I've just written one and I'd like to try it out on someone."

"Certainly, if you'd like," said the woman, a little astonished at the suggestion.

"Yes, do, please," said the daughter.

"Very well, then," said the Professor, and he told them "The Dream."

The Dream

Henry Adams had been an excellent Metropolitan police court magistrate. For five years before his retirement he sat at Marlborough Street, and that court had seldom known his equal. He was shrewd and quiet and had sufficient sentiment to make him human, but an equal fund of common sense to prevent sentiment taking liberties with his mind. He never courted popularity, but he was extremely popular both with his staff, with barristers and solicitors and, not least, with his regular clientele. If you met him from the dock you found him courteous and sympathetic, but not easily deceived. He knew when to be lenient and when to be severe. He was as painstaking with a regular customer, who had a cold and attributed her behaviour of the night before to an overdose of "that red wine," as he was with a serious charge of fraud. He never took a case for granted, but made certain that he had got to the bottom of it before he gave a decision. At the same time, he was quick minded and would not allow unnecessary hours to be wasted by irrelevant cross-examination. Longwinded barristers and senile solicitors found him extremely polite but equally firm in this respect. He saved much time by his habit of never interrupting unless it was essential to do so. Before his appointment he had seldom appeared in a criminal court. His practice at the Bar had been mainly commercial, and there had been some surprise and not a little pain at the criminal Bar when his appointment was announced. There were, at the time, several most estimable counsel who had prosecuted hundreds or thousands of criminals in the course of their career and who were, so to speak, queuing up outside the Home Secretary's office when the vacancy occurred. However, Henry Adams was appointed, and well he justified the Home Secretary's opinion of him. He had one other characteristic. He never intentionally said anything for the benefit of the Press. His few remarks were directed to the matter in hand and not towards furthering his views on birth control or the licensing hours.

Goldilocks – her surname varied and does not matter – on the other hand, was not a good girl. She was well known at Marlborough Street, where she usually appeared after she had sought custom with more persistence than discretion. Sometimes, however, she was charged with the more serious crime of robbing her customers after she had catered for their more immediate needs. Until Mr Adams became the magistrate her appearances in the court had usually been associated with some disturbance. Regular offenders usually fall into one of three categories: There is the person who says nothing except "Guilty" in order to be quit of the matter for better or worse as soon as possible. Then there is the man or woman who puts up some kind of defence, often in the end abandoned. There are numerous varieties in this second category, but they don't concern the present story. Finally, there is the third type, of which Goldilocks was at one time an excellent example. The members of this category are determined to make a scene. Sometimes they shout at the policeman while he is giving evidence; sometimes they abuse the magistrate; while sometimes they simply hold on to the dock rail and scream, continuing to scream long after their forcible removal to the cells. Goldilocks did all of these things in turn, and, when her case was called on, the court officials looked resigned and prepared for trouble. Mr Adams, however, knew how to deal with her. Before his arrival the usual procedure when she shouted out "Stinking lies" in the middle of the policeman's evidence had been to order her to be quiet, under the threat of a week's remand in custody. This merely provoked her to stronger and frequently repeated adjectives. They were frequently repeated because she had not a large vocabulary. She had spent a good many weeks in prison in this way. However, on her first appearance in front of Mr Adams, she was amazed when, following her allegations of "Lies, all lies," he turned to her with a friendly smile and said, "Well, tell me about them. Let's first of all see what is true in the constable's evidence, if anything. Will you help me?" This nonplussed Goldilocks, who was not used to this sort of treatment. She had not been listening to the evidence and merely called out "Lies" as a matter of habit. Consequently, when taken through the evidence very quietly by Mr Adams, she could not put her finger on any single false statement. "It looks as though you've made a mistake," said Mr Adams. "But don't worry, I shan't hold it against you. I only want to get at the truth, and you have helped me quite a lot, thank you."

Goldilocks remained silent for the rest of the evidence. When her turn came, instead of the usual outburst from the dock, she just said, "Oh, have it your own way; how much?"

"But I shouldn't dream of fining you until I've heard your story," said Mr Adams. "I know nothing about you. You may have done nothing illegal at all. There is nothing unlawful in speaking to strangers, provided you don't do it to annoy them or for immoral purposes. I only know what the policeman has told me. You may have quite a good explanation of your behaviour."

"You something well know I haven't," said Goldilocks sulkily, but not in her usual strident tones.

"I do, if you tell me so, but not otherwise."

"Well, I do; so there. Now get on with the job." Goldilocks obviously felt that something was required of her, but she had more than a suspicion that she was not living up to her reputation. Nor was she.

"Very well, then," said Mr Adams. "I must deal with the case on that basis and find you guilty."

The constable, who was still in the witness box, cleared his throat and began: "The defendant has been before this court …" He had not got any farther before the magistrate interrupted.

"Thank you, constable, but I don't want to hear of any previous convictions. The defendant has never appeared in front of me before and I shall treat her as a first offender." Goldilocks gasped.

"Are you trying to be funny?" she asked, after a pause.

"Not in the least," said the magistrate. "Go away and try not to come here again."

"But I've been here dozens of times."

"Well, we'll go into that next time, if there is one. Call

the next case, please."

And Goldilocks for the first time stepped demurely out of the dock, while the two policemen, who usually had the job of disentangling her from the rail, looked much relieved.

After that, on her numerous subsequent appearances, Goldilocks was a reformed character, in the sense that her behaviour in court was perfect. She stepped daintily into the dock, smiled at the magistrate, pleaded guilty and went daintily out to pay the fine. Her reputation at Marlborough Street as a difficult customer disappeared. She was the easiest of all. Only once there was a slight – very slight – passage of arms between her and Mr Adams. On her third appearance before him he said, "I suppose there's nothing we can do for you? The Court Missionary ..."

But Goldilocks interrupted him with "Now lay off that" and a toss of her head, reminiscent of her fighting days.

Mr Adams sighed, "Oh, very well, I'm sorry. Forty shillings," and the incident closed and was never repeated.

One afternoon the magistrate finished his work earlier than usual and decided to go home on the top of an omnibus. He joined a queue at the Regent Street stopping place. Suddenly a voice very close to him in the queue said, "Hullo." It was Goldilocks. This was an awkward predicament. Goldilocks looked very much what she was and, although his features were not publicly known, he was so close to his own court that he might easily be recognised, and it would not look well to be seen in conversation with her. On the other hand, to say nothing and turn the other way, as though he smelled bad drains, not only revolted his natural sense of politeness but, in his view, might have led to something in the nature of a scene.

You could never tell with Goldilocks. Bus queues have nothing to do and seldom have professional entertainers to while away their time. He could feel in his bones, in the split second before he made his decision, that the queue was also weighing up the possibilities of an enlivening incident. He said, "Good afternoon; where are you off to?"

"Ask no questions and you'll hear no lies," replied Goldilocks.

"I'm sorry," said Mr Adams. "It's hot, isn't it?"

"I don't know or care," said Goldilocks. "Is that the best you can do?"

"Well, you started this conversation. Isn't it up to you?"

"I only wanted to see what you'd do."

"What did you expect me to do?"

"Oh, I dunno, but it makes a change."

Just then another awkward predicament started to appear, in the person of the magistrate's clerk. He was approaching the queue. The magistrate made another quick decision. A taxi was passing.

He hailed it and jumped in with a "Goodbye, I'm in a hurry" to Goldilocks. Goldilocks also made a quick decision and jumped in beside him.

"Where to?" said the driver.

"Three times round the park," said Goldilocks cheerfully.

Seldom had the magistrate been called upon to do so much quick thinking about his own affairs. If he tried to eject Goldilocks from the taxi himself there would be an appalling scene and she would certainly bite him. If he called for a policeman, he might be well bitten before his arrival, and, in any event, there would still be a scene in front of his own clerk as well as the hundreds of people who would gather round. Moreover, the longer he stayed there the more likely he was to be seen in the taxi with her. He thought of jumping out himself and running for it, but this would not only be horribly undignified but the taxi had been hired and might pursue him for the fare.

"Go on, quick," he said to the driver, and off they went. He decided to wait until they reached a convenient place for disposing of Goldilocks and to spend the time meanwhile in trying to persuade her to get out quietly. He turned to her.

"Well," he said. "What do you want?"

"I'm very sorry," said Goldilocks. "It's very naughty of me. It was just a sudden thought. I wanted to go on talking to you. But I'll get out whenever you like. Do you like my legs?" she added.

"They're a very good shape," he said, "and I think they had better land at Hyde Park Corner, if that will suit you."

"You're very sweet," she said. "Why didn't you give me in charge?"

"Well, for one thing, you would probably have bitten me first."

"Oh, I never – well, perhaps – if I'm really angry – but not you – really not. I think you're ever so nice."

"Well, I couldn't tell that, could I? – and then I don't like scenes – and besides," he added, "I don't mind giving you a lift."

If Goldilocks had then said "You're a liar" she might have been right for once, but she didn't. She smiled.

"Don't you really? Oh, you are ever so sweet," and she squeezed his hand. The magistrate was getting pretty hot under the collar by this time, but he saw to his relief that they were approaching Hyde Park Corner.

"Stop by the hospital," he told the driver. A moment

later they stopped and automatically he got out to assist Goldilocks. Suddenly he jumped in again and almost shouted to the driver, "No – go on – 43 Bolton Gardens – quick." All that had happened was that he had just seen the Home Secretary emerging from the hospital. Had Goldilocks got out, the Home Secretary would have had a perfect view of Mr Adams assisting her to do so.

"You are funny," said Goldilocks. "I never thought you'd like me – dearie," she added. Her single track mind saw only one reason for Mr Adams' curious behaviour, and she got ready to make the most of her charms. She took his arm. "I don't," said Mr Adams; "at least not in that way." He was feeling very uncomfortable indeed. It seemed as though he were fated never to get rid of her. Now he had told the taxi driver his home address. He didn't suppose Goldilocks would bother him there – but she might – and, anyway, what was he to do with her when he did get home? He could just say "Goodbye" and give her some money perhaps. She would probably go quietly. He was rather sorry for Goldilocks. Whether he would have been as sorry for her if she had been older or less attractive is a matter of no concern. He probably would have been, but, in any event, he was sorry for her. She interrupted his thoughts. "That's all right, ducks," she said. "You needn't be shy with me; I understand; I'll show you a thing or two."

"No, you don't understand," he said; "you're quite mistaken. Be a good girl and take your arm out of mine."

"Then why did you keep me here?" He instinctively shirked the truthful reply, but he couldn't for the life of him think of another. At last he said, "Because I suddenly thought it would be a good idea if you came and had tea with me and my sister."

"I'm not having any missionaries."

"My sister isn't a missionary. You can just have tea and go away as soon as you like. Would you like it?"

"It'd be a change."

"All right, that's settled then." The magistrate relaxed. It seemed a simple solution, and it was just possible that his most understanding sister could do something for the girl. He hoped that she hadn't invited anyone to tea without his knowing.

In this he was lucky. It was his first piece of luck in the whole adventure, so he certainly deserved it. Everything after that seemed to go according to plan. His sister greeted Goldilocks as though she were a new member of the tennis club. Goldilocks behaved very well, and in due course, after an hour or so, she departed.

That should have been the end of the matter, except for Goldilocks' regular appearances in court, but Fate had not quite finished with the magistrate. This time Fate took the form of a most unattractive commercial traveller, who had charged Goldilocks with stealing. She always disliked being charged with stealing. It was not simply that it meant prison. She was probably honest by nature and it made her angry when her mode of life caused her to act differently. She had only once previously been charged with stealing before Mr Adams, and then he acquitted her for lack of evidence. This time the evidence was fairly conclusive, but Goldilocks fought very hard. All might have been well if the commercial traveller had not been permitted to cross-examine Goldilocks when she gave evidence. He enraged her and she started to slip back into her old ways – shouting her replies and using bad language. The magistrate decided to take a hand.

"Now, behave yourself," he said, "and answer the questions. The prosecutor says you took his wallet while you were in the taxi. Did you?"

"No, I didn't," she shouted. "I'm not a thief. I didn't

take anything from you when you took me in a taxi, did I?" It was out. She hadn't meant to say anything of the sort, but now that she'd said it her anger with the commercial traveller became confused with her anger at saying something she never meant to say. She lost all control.

"You're a nice one to try me," she went on. "Taking me out in a taxi, and then back to your home. That's not lies is it?" And she turned fiercely on the magistrate. He said nothing for a moment, thinking hard. He could not there and then state what happened. He could not simply deny the statement. He could not just ignore the question and proceed as though it had never been asked. There had been complete stillness in the court since Goldilocks' last threatening question. He could see the reporters waiting with their pencils poised. He was at a complete loss. There was no satisfactory solution. Eventually he said, "The fact that my sister and I entertained you to tea is nothing to do with this case. Go on with your evidence."

"Your sister and you," said Goldilocks. "That's a likely story, isn't it? Perhaps your sister was in the taxi too – under the seat." There was nothing else for it.

"Remanded in custody until Monday," he said. "We'll go on with the case when you can behave yourself." Goldilocks was eventually removed, shouting and screaming, to the cells.

After the court rose he sent for the reporters. "Gentlemen," he said, "it was obviously impossible for me to say more in court, but I want to tell you the whole story now. I hope that, when you have heard it, you will decide not to report anything about the case, but, even if I could do so, I am putting no pressure on you in the matter. If, however, you decide to report the proceedings I feel that I must, in fairness to myself, ask you to report this interview as well; otherwise an extremely false impression might be given."

He then told them exactly what had happened. They were obviously sympathetic. The magistrate knew that many people had been spared additional suffering in the past by the failure of the Press to report their misdeeds. In his case he had done nothing wrong, but the consequences of such a report in the Press might be serious.

"I shall have to tell my chief," said the senior reporter present. "Otherwise, someone in court may try to sell the story and I shall be blamed for not submitting it."

"You must do whatever you think right," said the magistrate. "Thank you for listening." He spent a troubled night.

The next day it was in nearly all the papers. It was a perfectly fair report, both of the trial and the interview, but it was sensational. There was little other news at the time and it was eagerly seized on by hard-worked news editors to do duty until something better should turn up. Unfortunately, moreover, there had recently been a number of public scandals involving well-known men. It was accordingly with a sense of misgiving that Mr Adams called on the Home Secretary three days later.

"You will have to resign," said the Home Secretary. "I'm not suggesting for a moment that there's anything in the girl's story, but you behaved very stupidly." Mr Adams would have liked to have asked how the Home Secretary would have behaved, but he thought it better not to do so.

"I can't have magistrates going out with prostitutes in taxi-cabs for any reason. It makes your position impossible – as you have seen for yourself. Must I arrange for another magistrate whenever this girl appears at your court, or is she to be able to say to her Judge every time she's charged with soliciting, 'You took me out in a taxi'? You've seen for yourself what are the deplorable consequences of your well intentioned but incredibly stupid behaviour. I say again – I'm extremely sorry, but I can't alter my decision. You must retire on the grounds of ill-health as soon as this has blown over."

Mr Adams left the Home Secretary. In due course he sent in his resignation. He tried to return to the Bar, but his heart was not in his work and his practice hardly began to materialise. Soon it ceased altogether. He was eventually reduced to the most difficult and least paying forms of journalism. Even so, he made less than enough to live on. And then, one day, when he had no work and no money, he suddenly saw the walls of his court returning and he found himself sitting in his usual seat. Thank God, it was only a dream after all. "Thank God," he said again, almost out loud. He saw the court was empty. He must have fallen asleep while that drivelling old solicitor in the last case went on and on. He wondered what had happened in it. Then his clerk came into the court.

"What did I do in the last case?" he said. "I'm afraid I fell asleep, but I've had the most appalling dream."

"You're a naughty old man," said the clerk, "a very naughty old man to fall asleep like that."

"I don't think you ought to call me a naughty old man," said the magistrate, "but I'm so relieved, I can't be angry with you. Still, it's not very respectful."

"What a naughty old man you are!" repeated the clerk. "What a very naughty old man! – you can't sleep here – you can't sleep here," and, as he spoke, the walls of the court faded away and Mr Adams awoke from the dream he so often had – a dream in which the tragedy of his life became just a dream. A policeman was touching him on the shoulder. "You can't sleep here, old man," he said. "Come along now."

"Very well, officer," said Mr Adams, and, gathering himself together, he got up and shuffled away.

CHAPTER NINE

The Liberty of the Subject

Before he had finished, the train had started again. "Thank you very much," said the woman. "That was extremely kind of you."

"I hope you enjoyed it," said the Professor.

"Oh, very much," said the woman.

"Very much indeed," said the daughter.

"Can you tell us where we shall see it published?"

"I'm afraid I can't," said the Professor. "It all depends."

He had never thought of the idea before, but it suddenly occurred to him as a possibility. "I think I shall change the title to 'The Tunnel,'" he said with a smile. The woman smiled back.

"I know," she said. "It's dreadful of me, but I just can't help it. It nearly drives me mad sometimes. One of the things I say to myself is – if you let it drive you mad you'll be locked up in a lunatic asylum and then you'll be worse off than ever. I can't think of anything more horrible than that, can you?"

"I certainly can't," said the Professor. "I should always give such places a wide berth."

They duly arrived in London and the Professor went at once to his friend's flat in Knightsbridge. Again he was in luck and found him at home. He confided his troubles. His friend was very sympathetic and understanding. "You can stay here, if you want," he said.

"No, I won't do that. It might get you into trouble. I'll stay until tomorrow, if I may, and then if you'll get some money from the bank and lend it to me, I'll go off. Really I shall enjoy it – provided I don't get caught. It's not as though I were committing a crime either, and I'm sure if I can once get rid of the certification I shall be all right again in no time. The very thought of going back to Tapworth House or some similar establishment is enough to cure me."

"I can't see anything wrong with you myself," said his friend. "What are those stories you tell? Are they any good, and where d'you get them from?"

"Some of them aren't bad," said the Professor. "They vary, of course, but where I get them from I really don't know. They just seem to come."

"Have you got one fit for my innocent wife?"

"Oh – certainly, there's nothing Rabelaisian about them at all."

"Tell us one after dinner."

"If you'd really like it," said the Professor.

"We would," they said. So after dinner the Professor told them "The Liberty of the Subject."

The Liberty Of The Subject

One of the most curious cases I have conducted started in the most ordinary manner. When I was first briefed, and, indeed, right up to the judgment, I would have been amazed if I had been told that one day I would write about it as a curious case.

I was briefed for the plaintiff Alfred Smirke, who was bringing an action for false imprisonment. Mr Smirke was a gentleman of somewhat doubtful antecedents, for whose quickness of mind and eye I had some admiration, but whose honesty I took leave to doubt. However, he employed a respectable solicitor, who paid me a satisfactory fee, and he told me no unnecessary lies. Indeed that is hardly fair to him or me. He told me nothing which could be shown to be a lie. His story, though a little unusual, was consistent throughout. That I disbelieved his explanations of certain incidents is neither here nor there; as Dr Johnson remarked, it is not for a barrister to try his client; that is for the Judge or jury.

Before I go any farther I must mention one fascinating little habit of Mr Smirke. Whenever he said anything which indicated that he had got the better of someone or that he had been rather smart in some way, he would put his tongue in his cheek – literally – and his eyes would twinkle. I say it was a fascinating habit. It certainly fascinated me. It usually occurred when he had not only got the better of someone but had done it (as I believed) in highly dubious circumstances. I used to watch for this little habit of his and I formed my view of him accordingly. Now you see how right it is that barristers are not the judges of their own clients. My client's little habit, which I ascribed to ill-concealed pleasure at some piece of knavery, may have been entirely due to some complaint like St Vitus' dance. I happen to notice these things and have a suspicious mind. A psychiatrist would probably have said that it was due to some accident while he was out with his nurse. Who knows? It may have been. You can form your own conclusions.

Well, here are the facts of the case as told to me by my client and as they came out in court. One night, my client had just finished transferring the entire contents of a house in East London into a waiting furniture van when the owner of the house and furniture – a Mr Herbert – returned. He was not at all pleased at what he saw. He promptly arrested Mr Smirke and locked him in his cellar while he called the police. Unfortunately it was a little time before the police arrived and my client spent an hour in a damp and dirty cellar. He was then transferred to a cell in the police station. He came up before the magistrate next morning and after a week's remand was acquitted. His explanation was this: he did not suggest that he had any right to the furniture or that the owner had asked him to move it. He admitted frankly that he had never seen the owner before that night. He had simply gone to the wrong house. He had been asked by a friend in a street with a rather similar name to move his furniture for him. He had never been in the neighbourhood before. He had been given a key by his friend which most unfortunately fitted both houses. The week's remand was ordered to enable him to call the friend to corroborate his evidence. The friend did so. My client said he had tried to explain all this at the time of the arrest but the defendant wouldn't listen, while the policeman said he could tell it to the magistrate. Mr Smirke was not a removal contractor, but he did odd jobs and had borrowed the van from a small man in that way of business. That was also proved. It was a pity that Mr Herbert had been out when Mr Smirke called. He had gone away for the weekend and returned unexpectedly the night before he intended. Mr Smirke was doing the job at night as he had some urgent work to do next day and he'd promised both parties not to let them down. The magistrate dismissed the charge and Mr Smirke called on Mr Herbert to pay him damages. Mr Herbert said he'd pay him nothing, and added that his only mistake was not to have had Mr Smirke's friend in the dock as well. Mr Smirke consulted Messrs Rounce and Ponsonby, and they in turn consulted me. Having heard my client's story in my chambers I mentioned that it was an unfortunate coincidence that Mr Herbert happened to be away when Mr Smirke called. If Mr Smirke had had evil intentions he had chosen the right time. Mr Smirke put his tongue in his cheek and said yes it was a coincidence, wasn't it? I also said that, if I'd been the magistrate, I should have wanted to know who made the key and the lock belonging to the house of Mr Smirke's friend. I should also have wanted to know if the lock had recently been changed. Mr Smirke said he quite agreed; he would have wanted to know that too – but the magistrate didn't. Anyway, added Mr Smirke, with his tongue still in his cheek, as he was quite innocent in the matter, those further inquiries could not have resulted in any additional evidence being obtained against him. I said that that was as well, as no doubt Mr Herbert's solicitors would go into that matter now. They were welcome, said Mr Smirke.

"Now tell me," he said, "what are my chances of obtaining damages and how much am I likely to get?"

I told him that this would depend upon the Judge's view as to whether the defendant had reasonable grounds for locking him up. I told him that there were certain legal decisions which helped him, but that if the Judge thought that the defendant was morally justified in his action the damages would be only nominal – say, £5 or £10 at the most. The defendant would probably pay that amount into court and, if no more than that were awarded, the whole costs of the action would have to be paid by Mr Smirke – some £200. If, however, the Judge thought the defendant had been unreasonable, the plaintiff might get up to £100 damages and, of course, the costs of the action.

It would very much depend on what Judge tried the case. He had an even chance of getting reasonable damages if he had the right Judge.

"How much would you award if you were the Judge?" he asked.

"One farthing," I replied without hesitation.

"So would I," said Mr Smirke. Then turning to Mr Rounce's managing clerk, he said, "Issue a writ at once," and with his tongue in his cheek, he walked out of the room.

The case came on for trial before Mr Justice Larkins. He was a fairly talkative Judge with a pretty taste for publicity. Illustrated papers more than once contained pictures of Mr Justice and Lady Larkins in their charming garden at Barcombe. Sometimes the little Larkins would be shown as well. He was not a bad Judge from our point of view, but until I had opened the case I did not realise how strongly he felt about the liberty of an Englishman. I soon discovered, however, that it appeared that this was just the sort of case he had been waiting for, and throughout my opening address he did nothing but intersperse helpful comments. Accordingly, when my client went into the witness box he could do nothing wrong. In cross-examination the Judge stood over him like a mother protecting her young, and counsel for the defendant could make no headway at all. There was usually an interval of about half a minute between the asking of an awkward question and the plaintiff's reply. This interval was caused by the Judge suggesting to the defendant's counsel, either that he'd asked that question before or that it was a question the plaintiff couldn't be expected to answer, or sometimes even by the Judge saying to the plaintiff – "I suppose your answer to that is so and so?"

On these last occasions, the plaintiff having said "Yes," the Judge wrote down the full answer which he had himself propounded. But all this was nothing to what happened when the defendant went into the box. I had to ask him practically nothing.

The Judge cross-examined him as though he were a pick-pocket.

"You are an Englishman, I suppose?" he asked.

"Yes," said the defendant, "and my house is supposed to be my castle, but it wasn't that night."

Mr Herbert was just about as annoyed with the Judge at the trial as he had been with the plaintiff on the night in question.

"Don't be impertinent, sir," said the Judge, "or you will find yourself in a very serious position. Stand up and take your hands out of your pockets."

Then he asked him whether he thought it important that the liberty of the subject should be respected.

"Yes," said the defendant, "and his property."

"One thing at a time," said the Judge testily. "Mr Courthope" (counsel for the defence), "during the luncheon adjournment you might teach your client how to behave in the witness box."

"Very good, my Lord."

"Now, Mr Herbert, why didn't you listen to the plaintiff's explanation instead of locking him up in a cold and damp cellar? I think your client did say it was cold and damp?"

"Yes, my Lord."

"Yes, in a cold and damp cellar. Incidentally you are very lucky there is no claim for doctor's fees or personal injuries. He might easily have got rheumatism. How old is Mr Smirke?"

"Forty-two, my Lord."

"A very dangerous age for that sort of thing. Now, sir, will you be good enough to answer my question?"

"Which question, my Lord?"

"Will you kindly pay attention to what I am saying? Why didn't you listen to the plaintiff's explanation?"

"Well, my Lord, if you came home in the middle of the night and found someone carting all your furniture out of the house – would you?"

"Don't ask me questions, sir. Answer mine. I'm beginning to form a very unfavourable view of your client's evidence, Mr Courthope. I ask him a very simple question and he evades it. And it is not the first time – not by any means. I will ask you once more, and if you can't or won't answer I will assume you have none to give. Why didn't you listen to his explanation?"

"Because one doesn't ask burglars for explanations. You lock 'em up first and the explanations can come afterwards."

"So that is your idea of how an Englishman should behave, is it? That is English fair play, is it? Lock him up first and hear his explanations afterwards. I'll write that down. Lock him up in a cold and damp cellar first – d'you agree it was cold and damp?"

"It may have been a trifle – nothing to worry about."

"Did you consider at all whether it was cold and damp when you locked him up?"

"No, my Lord."

"Then why quibble about it? Really, Mr Courthope, this is intolerable. I shan't try to help your client any more. Continue with your examination."

And so it went on. I must give the defendant full credit for holding his own, but he couldn't do anything right as far as the Judge was concerned. The evidence was concluded after lunch, and there was just time for the defendant's counsel to begin his speech before we adjourned for the weekend. He could hardly say a word without the Judge interrupting.

"Are you seriously suggesting, Mr Courthope, that your client had the slightest grounds for acting as he did?"

"What else could he do, my Lord?"

"What else could he do? You're not entitled to ask me questions, but I don't mind answering. What else could he do? – take his name and address and investigate the matter in the morning. Ring up the police as well if he liked. The explanation in fact was an extremely reasonable one and on being checked would have proved to be true. But your client took the law into his own hands, and, subject to anything you may be going to say, he will find that an expensive proceeding. No man is entitled to keep another man in custody, even for a short time, unless he has the strongest possible evidence to justify him. In default of actual violence you cannot have such evidence without giving the man you wish to arrest an opportunity to explain his conduct. Your client never did this, and" (looking at the clock) "during the weekend adjournment I think he would be well advised to consider trying to come to terms with his opponent. I will say no more about that. Monday morning at 10.30."

And the court adjourned.

I need hardly say that I did not spend any time that weekend preparing for my closing speech. It was obvious that I should not be required to make one at all except on the amount of the damages. So I attended to other far more pressing matters. Monday came and the hearing was resumed. I should say that, during the interval, the defendant had refused to offer a penny more than the £10 paid into court, and so no settlement could be effected.

Nor would I have advised my client to take less than £100 and his costs.

Courthope resumed his speech and this time the Judge did not interrupt him at all. I assumed he had run down on Friday and had not yet recovered from the weekend. Courthope finished and I got up, expecting the Judge to say that he wanted to hear me only on the amount of the damages. To my surprise he said nothing. I thought he must be daydreaming, so I said: "Does your Lordship wish to hear me both on liability and damages?"

"Certainly," replied the Judge. "Do you not wish to succeed on the issue of liability?"

"Of course, my Lord."

"Then you had better address me on the subject or I may think that there is nothing to be said on your client's behalf."

I was amazed. However, I put together quite an effective little speech, full of the Judge's own statements on the previous hearing and judiciously sprinkled with "As your Lordship observed on Friday."

He did not interrupt me, and I at length assumed that all that had happened was that he had not liked my easy assumption that I had won the case and that he wanted to keep me in my place. I was quite prepared to play at that game and I left nothing of importance unsaid. When I sat down I felt that all would be well, although I must confess I was still a little surprised at the Judge's attitude. Two minutes after I had sat down I was not just surprised – I was thunderstruck, and so was my opponent. In a short five-minute judgment the Judge stated that, in his view, the defendant had acted perfectly properly and the plaintiff might consider himself lucky to have been acquitted by the magistrate. If the law compelled him to award some damages he would award a farthing, which was a farthing more than the plaintiff ought to have. The plaintiff would pay the whole of the costs of the action. Courthope and I looked at each other. Our thoughts were precisely the same. Had Larkins gone mad? It was absolutely incredible.

I turned round to my solicitor, who was looking white and breathing heavily, and whispered that I would see Mr Smirke in the corridor. Just then the usher brought me and my opponent a note from the Judge, asking us to come and see him in his private room when he adjourned. The only other case in his list was settled, so he rose at once and we followed behind at a respectful distance.

Courthope and I said nothing on the way to the Judge's room – we were so dumbfounded. We just looked queries at each other. We knocked at the Judge's door and he told us to come in. We did so.

"Now – come in and sit down for a moment," he said most affably. "I owe you both an explanation. You must think I'm mad. You mustn't tell him so, but I would really like to apologise to Mr Smirke for leading him so near to the promised land and then driving him away. It's only fair to you to tell you all about it. Have a cigarette?"

We had one.

"When I left the court last Friday I had made up my mind (as far as I properly could) to give the plaintiff £100 damages. That must have been obvious to everyone in court. Now I'll tell you the reason for my extraordinary *volte face*. On Saturday night I was reading in bed when I heard a noise coming from the library. It persisted, so I got out of bed, took a revolver, and went there. Sure enough there was a burglar making away with a very nice collection of stamps and other rarities which ought to have been locked up. I covered him and said, 'Don't make any mistakes. This is loaded and I know how to use it. Keep quite still and keep your hands up.' 'Anything else?' he said. I didn't reply and went towards the telephone. 'I mean it,' he said; 'aren't you going to say anything else?' 'Not to you,' I replied. 'I'm going to ring up the police.' 'Oh, very well,' he said. 'I shan't get very fat on that.' 'I don't know what you mean by that, but you'll get the ordinary prison rations.' 'You don't understand,' he said. 'May I explain before you ring up the police? It will save a lot of trouble.' 'Explain?' I said; 'you can tell the magistrate,' and then the recollection of something that fell from me in my official capacity last Friday struck me, and I said, 'What is your explanation for breaking into my house and stealing my property?' 'Breaking into your house – yes,' he said, 'but stealing – no. I'm very sorry to have caused you all this bother, particularly as I've got nothing out of it worth having. I write short stories, and I'm writing one in which a burglar comes face to face with a Judge in the Judge's house. Now I've never met a Judge before, and I got stuck in trying to work out the dialogue. I couldn't think how the Judge would react. Well, my wife said to me jokingly – "Why don't you try it on a real Judge and see what he says?" I thought it ridiculous at first and much too risky, but after a bit the idea started to appeal to me. It might be quite amusing; so I decided to do it. To be on the safe side I brought the unfinished story with me. But I really do apologise; it's inexcusably bad manners.'

"He then asked if he could lower his hands to produce the story. I let him do so and he handed it to me. It undoubtedly was a manuscript of a short story, quite reasonably written, and it stopped at a point where a judge found his house burgled. 'You can check up on me in the morning,' he said, 'or tonight if you like. My name is Such and such and I live at So and so and tonight I'm staying at "The Bull." '

"I telephoned 'The Bull' and he was staying there. I was extremely annoyed at being disturbed, but I felt I must let him go and he went – taking with him irreplaceable property of mine to the value of £500 or more. He did not go back to 'The Bull' and the police haven't been able to catch him. Now, perhaps, you understand why my views on the reasonableness or otherwise of detaining people underwent a change. Please keep this to yourselves, but I felt the least I could do was to let you both know. You can tell your clients I'm an old fool and don't know my own mind. You'd probably do that anyway."

Then he chatted about a few other things and we left.

I found my solicitor but not Mr Smirke. My solicitor told me he hadn't been able to wait. I was sorry, because he had certainly had a raw deal from the Judge, and, without betraying the old man's confidence, I wanted to show that I sympathised and to say something rude about the Judge. If he'd just lost his case it would have been nothing, but losing it in that way must have been exasperating.

It was six months later that I happened to run into Mr Smirke at a local country pub. I'd almost forgotten about the case, but the sight of him reminded me of it and I was glad to get the opportunity I had previously missed. I went up to him and he at once remembered me. I made the best explanation I could and said I was extremely sorry at what had happened.

"That's all right," he said. "What you lose on the swings you make up on the roundabouts," and he put his tongue in his cheek and his eyes twinkled. It was then that I noticed he had a companion with him. I began to think that Mr Justice Larkins might have been very interested to see that companion. At the same moment something prompted my client to remember suddenly that they had a train to catch. As they hurried away I reflected that, in view of the unsettled state of the law, as interpreted by Mr Justice Larkins, it might be unwise to detain them against their will. So, after walking to the door and watching their fast retreating figures for a minute, I returned to the bar and asked for another half pint. "Sorry, sir," said the barman, "too late." The liberty of the subject indeed!

CHAPTER TEN

The Catch. Part I

Next morning the Professor was provided with sufficient funds and clothes and he caught a train for a small town in Worcestershire. He had decided not to go to Scotland in view of his remark to the doctor at the home. He arrived between tea and dinner time and went straight to "The Bear," a small hotel to which he had been recommended by his friends. As soon as he walked in to the place he felt that the recommendation was justified. Notice was taken of him immediately – not the ostentatious notice which is sometimes paid to the new visitor in big pretentious hotels, but a quiet, helpful notice which made him feel that he was wanted and would be well looked after without being interfered with. He registered in the name of Mowbray. He had not thought about the name question until the moment for registration arrived, and then the only name which came into his head was the one which his real name suggested. He gave his address as that of his friends in Knightsbridge and he immediately wrote a letter to tell them what he had done. He wrote his letter in the lounge of the hotel. He had just finished it when a youngish man, who was apparently the proprietor, came up to him.

"I wonder if you'd care for a glass of sherry before dinner," he said. "I have some Tio Pepe, if you like as dry a wine, but I have several less dry wines if you would prefer one of them."

"A glass of Tio Pepe sounds very good," said the Professor, who had already decided he was going to like the hotel. He drank two glasses of sherry and went up to his room.

"This is delightful," he said aloud. The room was not large, but it was pleasantly furnished and looked out on to the charming garden. He had a bath and changed at leisure and eventually went down to dinner. The dining-room was a small room with the tables fairly close together, and the atmosphere was friendly. The waiting was done by some attractive young women, while the proprietor himself attended to the drinks. Most of the tables were full when the Professor went in, and he was given a table to himself from which he had an excellent view of everyone else.

He looked at the menu. Oysters, turtle soup, roast duck, a sweet and a savoury. The proprietor came up to him.

"D'you like the look of it?" he asked. "Or would you like something else?"

"If it is as good as it reads," said the Professor, "I should be …," he was going to say 'certifiable,' but the word stuck in his throat – and, even when he said 'mad,' he coloured slightly.

"I should be mad to try to improve on it."

"Well, I hope it comes up to expectation," said the proprietor. "Please tell me if it doesn't. Now – are you interested in wine at all?"

"I am very fond of a good bottle of wine," said the Professor, "but I am one of the few people of my age who admit to knowing nothing at all about it. As a young man

I used to pretend that I knew quite a lot, but I have outgrown that form of conceit. I am quite content to put myself in your hands. I should have had to do so in any event, but I must confess that everything I have so far found in your hotel makes me do it most readily. I should like half a bottle of claret or burgundy, whichever you recommend."

"I think I can give you a wine you will like," said the proprietor. "If you don't like it, please say so and it will be changed."

The Professor began his dinner, and the wine did not have to be changed. Indeed, the Professor decided to treat himself to another half-bottle. He was extremely happy. He indulged in a little gentle badinage with one of the attractive young women who waited on him and he felt at peace with the world. He was drinking his coffee when one of the waitresses brought him a note. He saw from which table it had come. It was apparently from a young married couple. He opened it.

"WILL YOU PLAY WITH US AFTER DINNER PLEASE?" it read.

For a moment the Professor wondered if he were back in Tapworth House. He looked round the room – he looked at his wine glass and then he looked back at the note. Most extraordinary, he thought. He looked at the young couple, who were laughing together and studiously avoiding his gaze. He thought for a moment. Then he wrote on the back of the note, "WHAT DO YOU WANT TO PLAY?" and sent it to them. Back came the reply, "OH, ANYTHING, BUT DO SAY YOU WILL."

"ALL RIGHT," he answered, and having finished his dinner he walked into the lounge and awaited developments.

A few minutes afterwards the young couple came up to him, looking rather sheepish.

"Our name is Brown," said the man. "I suppose you think we're quite crazy."

The Professor got up.

"How d'you do?" he said. "I am James Mowbray. I certainly think you are both quite crazy, and I should like to hear all about it. Won't you sit down?"

They all sat down and there was a silence for a moment. The girl broke it.

"It's me, you know," she said.

She was a really lovely young woman and it would have taken a misogynist of a very determined character to resist her smile.

"We're on our honeymoon," she added.

"Then," said the Professor, "you must indeed be crazy. You look supremely happy and I hope you are."

"Oh – we are," they said together.

"Then I cannot understand your wanting the company of a third person."

"It's like this," said the girl. "We've had a little too much to drink, and I act on impulses when I'm like that."

"Well – what was the impulse on this occasion? If you had thrown your arms round your husband's neck in public, I could understand it, but I confess – I don't follow your idea at the moment."

Well – you'll think we're very stupid, but it's this. We're nearing the end of our honeymoon, and, of course, we want to be alone. But it's rather nice, we find – that is, I find …"

"We find," put in the man, "we find – it's rather nice to be prevented from being alone – just for a little – particularly after dinner. Then, when we do get alone again – it's all the nicer. D'you think we're mad?"

"Yes," said the Professor, "I do – but I understand your form of madness."

"Usually, George gets caught by somebody in the bar, but tonight he hasn't found anyone. We were just thinking that there would be no one at all when I saw you. I said to George 'Let's ask him to play,' and he said 'Yes.' I did tell you we'd had quite a lot to drink, didn't I?"

"Oh, yes," said the Professor, "you told me that. Well – now we're all here, what would you like to play? Do you know any games for three?"

"We hoped you'd be able to suggest something," said the girl. "It needn't be a very long game."

"Quite a short one would do," said the man.

"So long as we don't know when it's going to end," said the girl.

"I tell you what," said the Professor. "I'll tell you a story. How would that be?"

"Oh – lovely," said the girl. "Wouldn't it, George?"

"Very kind indeed," said the man. "Will it be terribly boring? Don't think I'm being rude; if you follow our complaint the more boring the better."

"I quite understand," said the Professor, "and I'll do my best to bore you, but I can't promise. Let us go over there where I shan't disturb other people."

They moved across to an empty corner of the lounge and the Professor began "The Catch."

The Catch (Part 1)

Mrs Lordan-Palfrey sat in the lounge of a big London hotel. She was, for the moment, alone. This was a rare occurrence. Fabulously wealthy, good looking, not yet too old, at the age to which she admitted, born into good society and acquiring by her own personality an important

120

position in it, she was not likely to be alone for long. She had entertained some of the best-known people in the country. She had even stayed with Hitler in the days when he was being appeased. There were few people of any note who had not attended at least one of her dinner parties, and there were no people who like that sort of thing who would not have given a great deal to attend one. She was good company and reasonably intelligent, but the quality in her most noticeable to those who knew her well was her obstinacy. If she wanted anything – which, strangely enough, was often – she would persevere until she acquired it. If she were determined not to do anything it was useless to try to compel her. If, as every man and woman is believed to have, she had her price, it was far too high for the ordinary mortal and she would have insisted upon payment in advance. It is very doubtful, however, whether the general rule – if there is one – applied to her. She had a husband, but at the moment he was big game hunting. Although quite fond of him she was by no means lost to the attractions of other men, nor were they lost to her many attractions. She was conscious of the position she held in society and enjoyed it. Accordingly she was very discreet in her indiscretions.

She sat enjoying her few minutes alone, and watched the other people. She was just imagining life in a semi-detached house in Balham – the coat and hat of a Marchioness whom she did not like had inspired the thought – when she was interrupted.

"Good afternoon," said a pleasant-looking young man of about thirty. She could not place him, and showed it when she replied with a query in her voice "Good afternoon?" She knew, of course, that she had met hundreds or even thousands of men whose faces she could not remember. She also knew that it was not uncommon for a complete stranger to take advantage of this fact.

"You don't remember me?" said the young man. "I told you at the time you wouldn't and you assured me you would. I'm very hurt, Mrs Lordan-Palfrey."

"Maybe," she answered without much cordiality, "but if you tell me who you are it would simplify matters." She had a feeling that she was being played with and she did not like being played with – not in that way.

"Well, of course," said the young man, "but I must whisper it."

"I see no reason at all for that."

"Ah, but you will when you hear." Then he bent down and whispered, "I'm a young man who wants £100." Then he straightened himself and added in an ordinary tone, "Now you remember, don't you?" Mrs Lordan-Palfrey did not answer immediately. Many thoughts raced through her brain. She had certainly never had anything to do with this young man before. Of that she was sure. She might have met him casually. Nothing more. Neither he nor anyone else had ever asked her for £100 – except, of course, for some charity. Charity? Good heavens! – perhaps this was the latest way of touting for contributions. Disgraceful. She'd soon put a stop to that. Then, suppose it wasn't charity? She had, she supposed, done things in her life – things the knowledge of which might seem worth £100. But she was not going to be blackmailed. She was quite determined about that. If this were charity she would expose it quickly; if it were blackmail she would have the young man put away for several years. She would quite enjoy giving evidence. Evidence. Yes – there must be more than her word for it. If she just called the porter and told him to fetch a policeman, the young man would deny the conversation and that would be that. No money had passed and it would be merely her word against his.

"I think I do remember – now you mention it," she said. "Won't you sit down?"

"Well, I mustn't really stop," said the young man, "but I will, just for a moment."

He drew up a chair close to her and sat down. "I was sure you wouldn't forget," he said. "How much can you let me have now?"

"It's very silly of me," she said, "but although I know you perfectly well – I can't quite place you."

"Anthony Spurling."

"Oh – yes, of course."

She must act quickly. Someone would be bound to come and interrupt them soon and she wanted to land this fish herself. It was a novel experience. There was this too. Just supposing the young man did know something. If she gave him in charge at once he might blurt out things which could quickly be spread all over the papers. On the other hand, the police had ways of dealing with such situations. If she could trap him into an interview in her own house she could see the police first and they could arrange everything. She had read about such things. Microphones, detective inspectors in grandfather clocks – they had a grandfather clock, but it was rather old and a burly policeman might spoil the inside – it had better be microphones. Her heart was beating quite fast in her excitement. She hoped she was not showing it. Anyway – it didn't matter if she did. He would think she was just frightened – frightened – yes, that was the cue. If she appeared too self-possessed he would be suspicious. Victims of blackmailers were always terrified.

"What – what – will you do?" she stammered just a little – she didn't know she was such a good actress. "What will you do – if I don't – if I don't …"

"Oh – please, Mrs Lordan-Palfrey, don't let's talk of that – so very unpleasant – and what is £100 after all to you?"

There was no doubt about it. This was no new charity scheme. It was plain blackmail. Now I wonder what he's got hold of, she thought, or is it just bluff?

She leaned slightly towards him and spoke very softly. "What is it you know?" she asked.

"Need we go into that?"

"Well – I must know what I'm paying for, mustn't I?"

"Well – I know everything."

Everything, she thought. What rubbish! He couldn't possibly. But still it was difficult to think he could know nothing at all. Keeping her voice still lowered, she said, "Is it about …?" and, without finishing the sentence, she looked meaningly at him.

"Mrs Lordan-Palfrey – or may I call you Helen – your name's such a mouthful isn't it?"

"By all means call me Helen if it will lower the price."

"Helen – don't be silly, then. When I say I know everything, I mean everything – not everything that's ever taken place in your life – of course not – but everything about one certain something …" He paused. "Need I say any more?"

She saw some figures approaching her and there was no time to be lost.

"Come to tea tomorrow afternoon at four o'clock and I'll give you the balance. Here's all I can manage now."

She dived into her bag while she was speaking and handed him a wad of £1 notes. He put them quickly in his pocket.

"Hanover Square?" he asked.

"Yes, of course."

"Well – goodbye – I shall love it. I must fly now," and he walked quickly away, just in time to avoid some old acquaintances of his victim. Safely away from the hotel he counted the money – £12 in all. Inside the hotel, while pretending to answer inquiries about her husband, her health and other matters in which neither she nor the questioners were in the least interested, she was also trying to work out how much she'd given him. Money meant nothing to her, but if he had made – let me see, was it £11 or £12 she'd given him? – out of her and did not come to tea, she would be very angry indeed.

As soon as she could she made her excuses and went to the telephone. She rang up a great friend of hers who was able and allowed to do most things for her, though his dividends were very small.

"Charles," she said, "I want to see the Commissioner of Police at once. Can you arrange it? Yes, this afternoon. Have I made myself plain to you, Charles? This afternoon. Thank you so much, Charles. You really are kind to me. I'll wait here for your call. Au revoir."

While she was waiting she suddenly became convinced that she would never see the young man again. I'm an idiot, she thought; £12 for five minutes' conversation is good business. He won't risk trying for any more. I'm a fool. But perhaps he will, though. Blackmailers are greedy. They always come for more. And he got it so easily from me that the temptation must be irresistible. Unless, of course, he suspects. Was it too easy? Then again, what was the "certain something"? In reality there were two "certain somethings" in her life which would not look well on the front page of the *Daily Mail* – even if she were referred to as Mrs X. But she would not be referred to as Mrs X. She would go right through with it. After all, she hadn't committed a crime. She had done what she had done, and if necessary she'd take the consequences rather than let Mr Anthony Spurling (or whatever his real name was) get away with it. Such infernal impudence too. To walk up to her at a London hotel and calmly say "I'm a young man who wants £100." He was certainly cool enough about it – though he moved quickly once he had the money. He wouldn't move so quickly next time, she reflected, or even if he did he wouldn't get very far. If only he comes, she prayed. She was called to the telephone. It was Charles.

"You darling," she said, when she'd heard the good news. "I'll meet you there at once."

Two minutes later she was in a taxi on the way to Scotland Yard. She met Charles outside and they were shown in almost immediately to the Commissioner. Charles had certainly arranged things quickly. As a matter of fact, if he has really important business, it is easy for quite an ordinary individual to see high officials at Scotland Yard at very short notice. So if you happen to be an Under Secretary of State, like Charles, the Commissioner is well within your reach. That is, if he is there. And he was there. Charles introduced Helen and was then very sweetly but very firmly asked by her to leave. As soon as he had gone, the Commissioner asked what he could do for her.

"I'm being blackmailed, Sir Maxwell," she said, "and I want your help and advice."

"You shall have both, Mrs Lordan-Palfrey. Of all crimes it is the most loathsome, and nothing gives me more pleasure than to save people from becoming its victims."

"I felt sure that was so. That is why I came at once. It only began half an hour ago."

"You certainly haven't wasted any time. If only everyone were as sensible a great deal of unnecessary suffering would be avoided. Now tell me about it. You can speak to me in complete confidence."

She told him what had happened. When she had finished the Commissioner spoke to Superintendent Hawksley on the telephone.

"Blackmailers, Superintendent, please. Age about thirty – well spoken – hotel worker. Soon as you can, please. Yes, in my office."

"I really must congratulate you, Mrs Lordan-Palfrey," said the Commissioner, while they were waiting. "You've done everything I should have asked you to do if we'd known it was going to happen. It's just possible that he's only in a small way of business and will be satisfied with the £12 – but I doubt it. In any event, it was a risk you had to take. If you'd panicked and called for the police at once we should have got nowhere. As it is, we'll have everything fixed up for tomorrow afternoon and with any luck we'll make a perfect capture. By the way," he added, "you haven't told me and I haven't asked you yet what knowledge, if any, you think Mr Spurling has. If it would embarrass you it's quite unnecessary to tell me now, but it may become necessary later."

"Sir Maxwell, I suppose there is no one whose whole life is a pattern of virtue. I do not claim to be an exception to the rule. If, however, as you suggest, my confession can be delayed, I should prefer that. Apart from anything else, I might tell you something of which he has no notion. I don't see why I should give myself away like that to you, Sir Maxwell."

"I quite agree, Mrs Lordan-Palfrey. We will wait and see what Mr Spurling says."

"And you mustn't get the idea that I'm a very wicked woman, because I'm not. There are just some episodes in one's life which one prefers not to share with the world at large."

"Exactly. Ah, here is Superintendent Hawksley. This is Mrs Lordan-Palfrey."

"How do you do?"

The Commissioner repeated the story to the Superintendent and then said, "Now, Superintendent, who have you got for us?"

The Superintendent produced a book of photographs and turned over the pages.

"I thought of Silky Jackson," he said, as he stopped at one page.

"No," she said, "he's much better looking. He hasn't got what I call a criminal's face, though I don't profess to be a judge. If I weren't prejudiced I should say he looked quite pleasant."

They went through that book and several others, but with no result.

"Well – never mind," said the Commissioner. "We'll worry about that side of it if he doesn't come to tea. We'll concentrate on tomorrow's performance now. I shall put Superintendent Hawksley and Chief Inspector Standring in charge. They will make all the arrangements with you for putting microphones in and they'll advise you which is the best room for the interview. I'm giving you them because I know that there is no one here more capable."

"It's very good of you."

"Not at all. I hope it will be a success. Put yourself in Superintendent Hawksley's hands and do exactly what he says, but don't hesitate to come and see me again if I can help you."

"That is kind of you. I'm extremely grateful."

"Don't mention it, please. Good afternoon."

"Good afternoon, and thank you."

She went out with the Superintendent and he arranged to call at her house at Hanover Square the next morning. She went home highly excited with her adventure. She had had several thrills in her life, but this was a new one. She did not sleep at all well for thinking of it.

Next morning the Superintendent and the Chief Inspector and several of their subordinates arrived at Hanover Square. They chose a room which did not lead to another, to avoid arousing suspicion. They almost filled it with microphones, which they cunningly concealed everywhere. They wired them up to a nearby room and tested them for sound. They could not miss normal conversation in any part of the room. The Superintendent then handed her £50 in £1 notes, which were not consecutively numbered.

"Now take it quite easily," he said. "Don't force the conversation or he may suspect. These gentlemen are sometimes shy birds. Let it come naturally. And don't forget we must have some reference to a threat before you hand over any money. Once he actually has the money on him say, 'Well, Mr Spurling, I hope you won't trouble me any more.' That will be our cue to come in, but do remember not to say it until he actually has pocketed the money. We don't want him to have a chance to put it down quickly."

"I understand, Superintendent. I think I can do it – if he comes, that is."

"Oh, he'll come, Madam. They always come, and come again. Now we'll be here at two o'clock just in case he comes early."

"Thank you very much, Superintendent. Would you care for a drink before you go?"

"Not on duty, thank you, Madam. Though if we catch the gentleman I shouldn't mind one then – if the offer is still open."

"You certainly shall."

Scotland Yard left and Mrs Lordan-Palfrey tried to amuse herself in various everyday affairs, but she was much too excited to think about anything else. She was really going to accomplish something. "Just imagine how many other people I may be saving," she thought. She had an early lunch and waited impatiently for things to happen. Scotland Yard duly arrived and took up its appointed position. She told the butler that she was expecting a Mr Spurling at four o'clock and that they would have tea in the study. All was prepared. But would he come? "Oh – please, please come," she said half aloud.

He did come. Punctually at four o'clock the butler showed him into the study where Mrs Lordan-Palfrey was waiting.

"Helen, how are you?" said Mr Spurling. "I'm so glad I could come. What a lovely dress! Do stand up and let me see all of it."

In the room near by Superintendent Hawksley was looking at the Inspector.

"So it's Helen, is it?" he said. "I thought there was something more in it than she told us. These birds never tell you everything."

Mrs Lordan-Palfrey was herself a little taken aback by the warmth of Mr Spurling's greeting.

"You can see it after tea. You're not a dress designer by any chance?"

"Oh, dear no, but I love beautiful things." He looked around the room. "What a charming room, too; it just suits you. You write your letters here I suppose?"

"Sometimes."

This was not quite what she had expected, but she reminded herself that she must take it easily, as the Superintendent had advised. She mustn't force the pace.

"I like that head," he said, indicating a picture on the wall. "It has great character. I'm not surprised that the artist wanted to paint it."

"It's one of my brothers. A cousin of mine did it."

"I can see you're an artistic family. Did you hear Toscanini the other night?"

Music was not a strong point with Mrs Lordan-Palfrey, but Toscanini was a social event and she had been there.

"Yes, I did, as a matter of fact."

"Well, I suppose it may be a dreadful thing to say, but I preferred Beecham's rendering of the 'Jupiter' to his."

"Really? You must be very musical."

"I'm very fond of it, but I speak with the confidence of the ignorant."

The maid brought in the tea. Meanwhile Scotland Yard was fidgeting.

"I could have had a day off today and seen the Arsenal," said the Inspector. "It looks as though I'd have done as much good there."

"Don't be too impatient," said the Superintendent. "Mark my words. This is a sly customer."

"There's a subject I'd like to mention," said Mr Spurling a little later, "but I know I shouldn't really."

Scotland Yard ceased fidgeting. Mrs Lordan-Palfrey's heart started to beat faster as she said quite calmly, "Oh, yes?"

"Yes – your scones, they're simply delicious. How are they made? I know it's vulgar to talk about food, but I must admit I'm very interested in it. Food, music, literature, art and lovely, intelligent women – I don't know which I like the best. Oh, and I forgot tennis."

"Do you find time for them all?"

"Not as much as I should like. I'm a hedonist. I want to do nothing but enjoy myself. At the same time, funnily enough, I want to see other people enjoy themselves too. That's why I want the recipe for the scones."

"Perhaps that's also why you came to tea today?" Mrs Lordan-Palfrey could not resist the retort.

"Well, no – I can't say that. I was thinking of myself today, I confess. Two of my wants are being catered for admirably. May I tell you that you're looking charming?"

"I can't stop you, but did you really come here to pay me compliments?"

She was getting a little tired of this waiting game.

"Not compliments, Helen, please. Compliments are insincere. I really think that you are a lovely, intelligent woman – and that your scones are excellent. Do give me the recipe."

Even the Superintendent was now getting a little restless. But he had not been in the Force twenty-four years for nothing. He could wait. He enjoyed pitting his brains against someone else's, and he had the comfort of not knowing that his were often far inferior to his adversary's. All the same he would have liked to have been a little nearer to the expected developments. However, after a further half-hour of cross chat, Mr Spurling said that he must really be leaving now.

"I haven't an engagement," he said, "but I'm a country man by nature and I feel cramped in London, sort of claustrophobia. I sometimes feel I must go for a walk in the Park. It's the one place where I can really feel free in London. Do you ever feel like that?"

"I can't say that I do. I like walking in the Park, of course, but I never feel any violent urge to go there."

"Ah, you're a town dweller, that's obvious. You wouldn't care to go for a stroll, I suppose, say, tomorrow morning?"

"I'm not sure whether I can."

"I think it's so lovely to wander across the grass or down by the Serpentine, particularly if I have a lovely or even just an intelligent woman with me. Do say you will. One can talk so much more freely, I find. There's less sense of restriction. Don't you agree?"

"I think I know what you mean."

"For instance, if we were walking in the Park, I should probably make violent love to you – now don't get agitated – only in conversation, of course – whereas here, where there's even a greater opportunity, with no one to see or hear, I merely talk nonsense."

"There isn't a greater opportunity here. I should just ring the bell."

"You're perfectly justified, Helen, in view of what happened last time. But I've kept my promise, haven't I? I haven't even tried to kiss you."

The Superintendent and the Inspector looked at each other again.

"I knew it," they said simultaneously.

"I don't know what you're talking about," said Mrs Lordan-Palfrey, painfully aware of what Scotland Yard must be thinking and blushing at the thought. All the same Mr Spurling was not going to get away with it. More than ever now she was determined to see him in the dock.

"She doesn't know what he's talking about," said the Superintendent.

The Inspector winked for answer. Mrs Lordan-Palfrey thought quickly and made up her mind. She must get rid of Mr Spurling before he said any more, but she'd meet him again – oh, yes, she'd meet him again – and again if necessary. She got up.

"Well, you'd better have your walk in the Park," she said, "and if you like to call for me, I'll go with you tomorrow morning."

"How sweet of you," he said, "but would you think it very ungracious of me if I suggested meeting there instead – say, at the Round Pond?"

"If you prefer it."

"Thank you, Helen. If I'd said that to a dozen other women they'd have been furious. But you really seem to understand me."

"I think I do," she said.

"Very well, then – goodbye until tomorrow – at, shall we say – eleven o'clock? – good – and thank you again for my tea."

She rang the bell and Mr Spurling left and was in due course shown out of the house.

When he was safely gone Mrs Lordan-Palfrey looked at herself in the glass and tried to remove the last remnants of her blushing with some powder. Unfortunately, however, the realisation of what she was doing recalled the conversation to her mind so vividly that she blushed again.

"Don't be absurd," she said to herself – but when she went to the room where the detectives were she had on her face the look of guilt which is often worn by an innocent person who knows he is believed guilty.

"I'm afraid that wasn't a great success," she said.

"That's all right, Madam," said the Superintendent. "He obviously suspected a trap from the start. He wants it in the open where he can make a getaway. That's why he won't call for you tomorrow. Meeting you in the Park he'll be watching you to see if you are being followed. You won't be followed, but we can deal with that all right. You'll take him as far away from people as you possibly can. We will keep our eye on him with field glasses and he'll be stopped when he leaves the Park, if he comes out alone. If you're with him, and it's worked, drop your bag. It's not so good as if we could hear the conversation, but he'll have to show how he came by the marked notes. If he says you owe it to him he'll have to do a lot of explaining and eventually we'll be able to show he's telling a pack of lies. Don't you worry, Madam, you can rely on us, and we're very discreet," he added.

Until he said that she had almost recovered. She immediately blushed again. "Thank you very much, Superintendent," she said. "Then all I have to do is to meet him tomorrow, give him the money, and you'll do the rest?"

"That's right, Madam, but you must ask him what he'll do if you don't give it to him, before you part with it."

"I quite understand. Thank you very much. Good afternoon."

She would have offered him a drink, but that "We're very discreet, Madam," still sounded in her ears. "I'll give Mr Spurling 'very discreet,' " she said to herself. "I wonder what the maximum sentence is. I must find out."

She did. It is penal servitude for life. That did her quite a lot of good. She went to a cinema that evening. When she saw shots of Scotland Yard and the CID at work the thrill of the chase started to replace her annoyance at being made to look ridiculous. She wanted to say to the friend who was with her, "I was there yesterday. I know all about their methods; d'you know I've got £50 in notes on me now – actually handed to me by Scotland Yard?"

But she said nothing. She would wait till she had won before she mentioned it to her friends.

Again she passed a fairly restless night and waited impatiently until it was time to go. She drove to Lancaster Gate Station and started to walk from there. He came up, smiling, as she reached the Round Pond.

"Punctual as ever," he said to her. "How are you?"

"It's quite unnecessary to keep up this farce," she said. "I know what you want and you know what I want. We'll go somewhere where I can give it to you."

"Really, Helen," he said. "You do put things crudely."

"I shall continue to do so."

"Well, do avoid such embarrassing expressions. I went quite hot under the collar."

"I'm not prepared to discuss my choice of language with you. Where would you like to go?"

Before he could answer they were accosted by Mary Sugden, a friend of Helen's. They were quite good friends when they did not both want the same thing. When that happened they were like most women who are not entirely unselfish.

"Hullo, darling," said Mary. "Have you brought your boat?"

Mrs Lordan-Palfrey was not pleased, but there was nothing for it.

"Oh – hullo – Mary, no – not today."

"I haven't seen anything of you for weeks. Where have you been hiding?"

"Nowhere, but I have been rather busy. We must meet for lunch one day. What about Tuesday?"

"I say, you know," said Mr Spurling, "you haven't introduced me."

136

Mrs Lordan-Palfrey stifled the reply she wanted to make.

"This is Mr Spurling," she said, "Miss Sugden." They shook hands. They had previously taken each other in at a quick glance and they had both been quite pleased at the result.

"I'm afraid I can't manage Tuesday, dear. But come round for a drink before lunch today. I can't ask you to lunch, I'm afraid."

Mrs Lordan-Palfrey replied automatically, "I should love it," and cursed herself the next moment, because she knew what was coming.

"And bring Mr Spurling with you."

"Thank you, I should love it too," he said.

"Well, that's splendid. Now I must fly. Dick is making frantic signs to me."

"Who's Dick?" he asked, when Miss Sugden had left.

"Nothing to do with you," she said. "Will you please understand that my acquaintanceship with you is purely a business one. I wish to have nothing whatever to do with you apart from that business, and I wish you to have nothing to do with me or my friends. Is that quite clear?"

"You're very unkind to me, Helen," he said. "Am I as bad as all that?"

"I can think of few things worse than blackmail," she said, "and if you weren't a blackmailer, I should still want to have nothing to do with you. Now where shall we go and get this over?"

"Helen," he said, "you are very stupid for an intelligent woman. Or else you think me very stupid."

"What do you mean?"

"Do I really need to explain?"

"Yes."

"All right then. Let's take a stroll while I do."

They walked away from the Round Pond on to the grass, wandering apparently aimlessly, while he talked. Anyone seeing them would have imagined that they were lovers or at least intimate friends. As a matter of fact, someone did see them – none other than Archibald Blackett, a close friend of hers. He could not place Mr Spurling, and wondered who he was. Helen ought not to wander in the park with a young man while her husband was away, unless the young man happened to be Archibald Blackett. He made over to them.

"Go away, Archie," she said, when she noticed him ten yards away. "I'm busy."

"So it seems," he said, " but mayn't I say good morning to you?"

Mrs Lordan-Palfrey said nothing. She was very angry and did not want to show it too obviously.

"I don't think we've met before," said Mr Spurling. "I'm Anthony Spurling."

"How do you do? I'm Archie Blackett."

Oh – so you're Archie," said Mr Spurling. "Helen has told me a lot about you. I've hoped we should meet."

"She hasn't told me anything about you," said Archie.

"That's as well," said Mr Spurling, "or you'd have been prejudiced against me from the start. She doesn't like me very much."

"She seems to like you well enough to wander hand in hand with you among the daisies."

"Not hand in hand," said Mr Spurling, "unfortunately. I can assure you that any advances of that nature meet with no success. No – I'm simply helping her settle a problem. That done, I shall walk out of her to life."

"It sounds very intriguing. Do I know anything of the problem, Helen?"

"You know nothing at all, Archie. You never did know anything."

"Oh – come – I say – what have I done?"

"I'll tell you what the problem is," said Mr Spurling. "She has a debt of honour to an old friend of hers who is very poor but very proud. She wants to find a means of paying it to him without him knowing it."

"That should be simple enough. Pay it into his bank."

"He hasn't got a bank."

"Well, open an account for him."

"He'd refuse to draw on it."

"Send him the cash by post."

"He'd send it back."

"Well, if he's such a determined idiot, don't pay him at all."

"But she'd never be satisfied if she didn't, would you, Helen?"

She did not answer.

"Well, I give it up," said Archie, "unless you give it to charity instead – or to a friend of his who's hard up too."

"When you've both finished arranging my affairs for me," said Mrs Lordan-Palfrey, "perhaps you'll let me know. Archie, I'm seeing you at dinner tomorrow night. You can go away now."

"Oh – very well – but I don't know what's the matter with you."

"Well, the matter with you is that you're in the way. Do you understand that?"

Archie looked astonished at this outburst – then he raised his hat and walked away.

"I'm afraid I'm being rather a nuisance," said Mr Spurling. "But it's entirely your own fault for calling the police in. You're not at all a good actress. No one who is being blackmailed behaves with the ease you showed in Hanover Square."

"You have plenty of experience of blackmail then."

"I read quite a lot. It was obvious that the house was full of detectives – just as much as it's obvious now that you've got a bag full of notes that you're dying to hand over so that the police can pick me up with them on me. You know it's true. I ought to have warned you not to go to the police, but I didn't have time at the hotel. You've made things infinitely more difficult for yourself. You see that, don't you?"

"What d'you want me to do?"

"I'm not sure – you've made it so awkward. But, first of all, tell me this. It will save us both time. Are you determined not to pay any more? If so, just tell me straight out and I'll know where I stand. So will you after a few days. Is that the case?"

"I don't know," said Mrs Lordan-Palfrey truthfully. She was getting into very deep water.

"Well, you must make up your mind what you want to do. If you want to buy my silence you must pay me as and where I say and there must be no funny business with the police. If you won't pay, just say so. Now, which is it?"

"What do you know?" said Mrs Lordan-Palfrey.

"That you will find out if you don't pay. You are buying silence, not information."

Mrs Lordan-Palfrey was beginning to wish she'd called the police in at the hotel. It was becoming very different from what she'd expected. This young man was a very tough proposition – much too tough for her. It was all very well for the Commissioner to say she had done just the right thing. She wanted to cry, she wanted her husband, she wanted Charles, Archie, anyone who would take the man away and deal with the matter. But no one was there.

The realisation of this steadied her. She wasn't a fool and she wasn't a coward. She was not going to be bullied by Mr Spurling. She would still put him where he ought to be. Penal servitude for life, she said to herself.

"I'm prepared to pay. Tell me where and when and how much. I can't stand any more of this."

"That's better," said Mr Spurling. "But I'm not quite satisfied about you yet. We'll go for a drink at that Miss Sugden's and there I'll tell you where to meet me."

"Do you insist on going?"

"I insist on nothing, Helen. It's for you to decide what you want."

She turned towards Knightsbridge where Mary Sugden lived.

Cheer up," said Mr Spurling. "I can be quite good company and I won't disgrace you."

She did not answer:

"Now, it's no use taking it to heart," he said. "Make the best of everything. That's the easiest way. Now what would you like to talk about? I can be quite interesting."

"When you're in your cell doing penal servitude for life I'll get permission to come and look at you," said Mrs Lordan-Palfrey.

"There you go again," he said. "You make things so difficult for yourself. I haven't the slightest intention of going to gaol. Now that it's so obvious that you want to put me there, it means that I shall have to be more careful than ever. It may even mean that I shall have to leave you alone altogether, and content myself with writing a few anonymous letters and selling an article or two to the Sunday papers. That would be a pity if neither of us wanted it that way."

"I give in," she said, and it really sounded as if she meant it.

CHAPTER ELEVEN

The Catch. Part II

As the Professor said the last words he noticed that his audience had left him. He smiled. Charming children, he thought to himself. I will drink a glass of port to their health. And he did – a very good glass of port. Then he went to bed in a happy frame of mind. He slept excellently and was down quite early for breakfast. He did not see Mr and Mrs Brown until lunch. They smiled at him as they came in, but did not speak. After lunch, however, they came up to him in the garden.

"Please, Mr Mowbray," said the girl, "we're sorry. Will you finish the story now please?"

"Wouldn't you prefer it after dinner?" said the Professor.

"No – now, please," said the girl, "that is, if you don't mind – and if you've forgiven us for being so rude and running away."

"There's nothing to forgive," said the Professor. "D'you remember where I had got to?"

"Oh yes," said the girl. " We were very interested. In fact we weren't bored at all."

"Then I must be counted a failure," said the Professor.

"Oh no," said the man, "it was the length that did it. As a matter of fact we were talking about it on our walk this morning and wondering what was going to happen."

"You'd got to the point where they were walking across the Park to go to Mary Sugden's," said the girl.

"Then you really were listening," said the Professor. "Well – well – well. All right then, I'll start from there."

The Professor repeated the last few words which Mr and Mrs Brown had missed the night before and then went on:

The Catch (Part II)

They took a taxi to Mary Sugden's. Mr Spurling was introduced to a few people who were there, but he concentrated his attention on Mary Sugden. They liked each other from the start, and it was only the fact that she was the hostess that prevented them from retiring into a corner together and ignoring the rest of the company. Before he left he had arranged to take her out to dinner.

Shortly after he had done this, he said he must go. Then he said quite casually to Helen: "Don't forget, I'm calling for you on Wednesday night – seven o'clock."

"It was Wednesday, was it?" said Mrs Lordan-Palfrey. "I won't forget."

"You musn't be late or we'll miss dinner or the curtain-raiser."

"I'll be ready."

He said goodbye and left. Before leaving, Helen told Mary she wanted to speak to her privately. They went into another room.

"Is it about Anthony Spurling?" said Mary.

"It is."

"Well – I'm not interested. You're married and I'm not, and I've just as much right to go about with him as you have – more."

"Right to go about with him? My dear Mary, that's really funny."

"Well, I don't think it funny."

"All right, Mary, I resign. You have him. There. I can't say fairer than that, can I? Shall I send him round or will you take him with you?"

"You're being odious, Helen, and, although it suits you, I don't like it in my house."

"I'm very sorry. I withdraw. Let's forget it. But – seriously, he seems to have made a great impression on you in a very short time."

"Well – how long have you known him?"

"Now that you remind me – two days, so I suppose I can't talk. I must admit that he's made an impression on me, too. However, I won't be selfish. He's going to the theatre with me on Wednesday, but apart from that I promise to see as little of him as possible."

"Oh – you needn't do that," said Mary, who was beginning to feel she'd made too much fuss about a man she'd met for an hour. "I just thought he was quite nice."

"Well, I'll be interested to see how it turns out. By the way, have you ever done anything you're ashamed of?"

"Of course – haven't you? Why do you ask?"

"Oh, no reason really – I just wondered. Now I really must go."

She went straight home and rang up the Commissioner of Police. They arranged to meet at Charles' flat. It was possible that Mr Spurling would have both her house and Scotland Yard watched. They arrived soon after each other. Charles had told his housekeeper to let them in. As far as either of them could tell, they were not followed. She told the Commissioner everything that had happened.

"It's more difficult than I expected," he said.

"You've got to get him," she said. "I don't care what it

costs me, you've got to get him."

"I will do everything that can be done. Now, there's only one theatre with a curtain-raiser. He's pretty certain not to take you there, as he mentioned it. I can't supply detectives to go to every theatre in London."

"I can, if you think it would be a good idea. I've told you, I'll pay anything you like. You can hire all the private detectives in London if you like – fill all the theatres with them. Would £10,000 be enough to cover it?"

"Ten thousand pounds? He seems to have annoyed you, Mrs Lordan-Palfrey."

"Will it be enough? You can have more if you want."

"You're really serious then?"

"Never more serious."

"Very well, I will see what can be done. You must wear a dress which they can all recognise. A tiara would be a good idea. Let me know exactly what you will be wearing, and make it as striking as possible. If I can arrange it in time I will have detectives in the stalls and dress circle of every theatre in London. As soon as it is known in which theatre you are, all the detectives will come from the other theatres. I will distribute them in the restaurants to which you may go and have sufficient outside the theatre in cars and taxis to make certain that you can be followed. Carry out Spurling's instructions to the letter. Do exactly what he tells you. I will see that you're kept under observation all the time. If he suggests a drive in the country, go with him. Wear a distinctive flower in your dress, say, a red carnation. As soon as he has taken the money, remove it. He will then be arrested by the first detective who sees you without it. I can't promise success, but we'll have a very good try."

"Thank you very much, Sir Maxwell. I do hope you'll be able to bring it off. I'm getting a little tired of my tête-à-têtes with Mr Spurling."

"I'm not surprised. Now let me know what you'll be wearing and I'll do the rest."

Sir Maxwell left and she waited for Charles to return. He was allowed to cheer her up. They had a drink at the Berkeley, and, as they went out, they caught a glimpse of Mr Spurling talking animatedly with Mary.

"Who's that with Mary Sugden?" said Charles. "She seems to like him."

"I think his name's Spurling," she said. "I just know him."

"Not one of the Grant Spurlings, I suppose?"

"Possibly; I don't know."

She spent quite a pleasant evening with Charles. He was terribly kind and it was very comforting to be with him.

Wednesday came and she prepared herself for the new ordeal. This time she was no longer praying that he would come and excited at the great adventure. She would have been delighted if he hadn't come – delighted if she never saw him again. Then suddenly a surge of anger came over her.

"If he does come I will get him this time," she said to herself.

He called for her punctually and seemed in very high spirits.

"I hope you haven't seen 'Highway Robbery,'" he said. "I'm told it's good and the curtain-raiser before it is excellent. Where shall we dine?"

"Wherever you like."

"Very well, then, Boulestin. It's near the theatre and it's the only restaurant where they can make soup. Do you like soup?"

"Not particularly."

"Well, you'll like *Crème Reine* at Boulestin. Have you had it?"

"I wouldn't know."

"You don't take enough interest in things. You don't care for music or food. What do you like?"

"Oh, plenty of things. You won't think me unfriendly, I hope, if I say that I enjoy most things in the right company and few in the wrong."

"Like all of us. Very natural. Ah – here we are." They had an excellent dinner, extremely well chosen, and arrived at the theatre just in time. They sat in the stalls. Just before the curtain went up he said, "I suppose I'm not allowed to tell you how striking you look to-night. Like a real princess. You aren't one, are you?"

She did not answer. She hardly noticed what the play was about. She was wondering whether the woman next to her with the ugly hands was a detective or whether the heavy-breathing man behind them was one.

During the interval she was able to look round. The house was full. A number of highly intellectual people would have been much insulted had they known that they were suspected of being private detectives.

"You remember our discussion in the Park?" she said at length.

"I remember several."

"The last one."

"Oh, yes?"

"I was wondering when it was all going to end."

"Oh – there's plenty of time yet. By the way – you shouldn't have said that to me," he added.

"Why?"

"Talking of the Park has given me a nasty claustrophobic feeling."

She sat through the rest of the play in a frame of mind very like despair. She had failed again. She knew quite well what he meant. Was it never going to end? It was intolerable.

"Where would you like to go afterwards?" he asked.

"I think I'd like to go home."

"Not tired so early? Don't you think just an hour or so at Gelanos would be good? Don't if you'd rather not. We'll do whatever you say."

"Oh – very well – let's go to Gelanos."

"You don't sound very enthusiastic about it."

She smiled wearily.

"I'm doing my best," she said.

Now it so happened that the heavy-breathing man was one of the detectives and, within ten minutes of their conversation, every table except one had been booked at Gelanos. That one table was kept for Mr Spurling and Mrs Lordan-Palfrey.

Superintendent Hawksley saw the manager himself and explained sufficiently what was in the air. It was a good night for private detectives. They would like more jobs of that kind. The play ended and Mr Spurling and his partner drove to Gelanos. Seldom had there been such a gathering at that distinguished place. The place was filled with detectives of all kinds – some from the CID, some from private agencies. There were detectives among the waiters and attendants, too. The Commissioner was certainly doing it in style. They were shown to a table and sat down. They danced a little. She saw the Duke and Duchess of Glenmouth arrive. She heard the head waiter apologising for the absence of a table.

"Surely you can find something," said the Duke. The Duchess caught her eye and smiled. She smiled her best party smile back.

"Who's that?" he asked.

"Oh – just some friends."

"That I could guess. Are you ashamed of them?"

"Certainly not."

"Then what are their names?"

"It's the Duke and Duchess of Glenmouth, if you want to know. Now I suppose you want them to come and sit at our table."

"Exactly. How did you guess? You're certainly improving. Let's go and ask."

They danced across the room and Mrs Lordan-Palfrey went up to them.

"How are you? It's terribly crowded. Would you care to share our table? This is Mr Spurling."

"That's extremely kind of you. Won't we be intruding?"

"Not at all, please join us," said Mr Spurling. "Helen is lecturing me at the moment and you've come just in time."

They sat down at the table. The Duchess started to look around her.

"My dear," she said eventually, "have you noticed what extraordinarily dressed women there are here tonight?"

"No, I hadn't."

Mrs Lordan-Palfrey glanced round the room. It certainly seemed different from an ordinary night.

"They are a little dowdy, I suppose," she said.

"A little?" said the Duke. "I was told I should see a host of lovely women."

"Oh – don't you know what night it is?" said Mr Spurling.

They all looked inquiringly at him.

"Obviously you don't. Helen, you should have explained. This is a special night for the Detectives' Benevolent Association. Helen's a vice-president you know."

Mrs Lordan-Palfrey gulped and tried to take a quick drink, but her glass was empty.

"I should like some champagne, please," she said.

"I'm so sorry," said Mr Spurling, and beckoned to a waiter.

"Some more champagne, please, and ask that waiter over there to come here."

"Certainly, sir."

The second waiter did not appear to accept the order with the customary speed of waiters at Gelanos. However, there was nothing for it and he came up to Mr Spurling.

"You see," explained Mr Spurling, "they do like we did in the Army. Some of them dine and others wait. Now, which particular branch are you in?" he said to the waiter.

"I no understand," said the waiter. "I just a waiter."

"A waiter, my foot," said Mr Spurling. "You're a detective. Which agency d'you come from or are you CID?"

"I just a waiter."

"Sweet, isn't he?" said Mr Spurling. "He's so used to acting parts that he really thinks he is a waiter. Never mind – but you'd be much more effective if you really did some waiting instead of merely looking decorative and not very decorative at that. I've watched you for the last half-hour and you haven't done a thing except bustle about doing nothing. However, you have tried."

"Would you think me terribly rude if I went home?" said Mrs Lordan-Palfrey. "I've the most dreadful headache."

"Oh – why didn't you say so before, Helen? We wouldn't have come here at all. Or has it only just come on?"

"I feel rather faint," said Mrs Lordan-Palfrey. "I shall be better when I get home."

Mr Spurling summoned a waiter and paid the bill. They took their leave of the Duke and Duchess.

"If that was Helen's latest acquisition," said the Duchess after they'd left, "I think she's regretting the purchase."

"Didn't seem a bad chap," said the Duke.

"All the same, I don't think Helen likes him," said the Duchess. "Why do all the detectives come here? It seems a strange idea."

"I think he was trying to be funny. Look! there's George Drew just come in and his lovely young wife. That's better. Oh, and there's Banchester and his fiancée. That's better still. Why – look!"

He might well have said "look," because a kind of transformation scene was being enacted. In place of the dowdy came the glorious creations of Bruton Street. Within half an hour of Mrs Lordan-Palfrey's departure Gelanos was itself again.

"How extraordinary," said the Duchess. "I suppose they think the vice-president's gone on somewhere else and they're all following. She ought to have told them she wasn't feeling well. However, I expect they will have a good time. Why, how are you, Charles?" and she greeted a newcomer.

Outside, Mrs Lordan-Palfrey was being escorted home by Mr Spurling in a taxi. They appeared to be the leader of a convoy. At one stage Mr Spurling actually got out of the taxi, just before the lights changed in their favour, and gave the "advance" sign to the taxis and cars behind. Eventually, Mrs Lordan-Palfrey spoke: "I am going to speak to you in the language of the gutter," she said, "because I'm sure you can't understand any other. You are the filthiest swine I've ever met. You can publish what you like or write what you like – I'm never going to see you again."

"Helen," he said, "you've been overdoing it. I warned you before and this is the consequence."

He looked out of the window. "Silly idiots. They've taken the wrong turning. We'd better wait for them."

He knocked on the driver's window. "Just stop for a moment," he said.

The taxi slowed down and stopped. Mr Spurling got out. A car came round the corner. He halted it and spoke to the driver. "You missed us at the last turning. We're just moving now."

He got in again and the convoy moved off. "You're very foolish, Helen, not to take notice of what I said. You've just been squandering your excellent money, which might have been used for far more useful purposes. Why didn't you trust me?"

"Trust you?" she said. "Trust you? Are you mad or what? You force money out of me, demand more and then suggest I should trust you. My only fault was to give you anything in the first place."

"That was certainly your first mistake – but, having done that, you made another mistake in going to the police. I can't so much blame you for that, as I hadn't warned you, but to go to them again, and yet again, after I had warned you, was madness – as you now see. Much better to have trusted to my chivalry."

"Chivalry? Am I dreaming – or did you say 'chivalry'?"

"Well – here we are, safe and sound at Hanover Square. So we needn't discuss it, need we? No – I won't come in and have a drink, thank you. By the way, I'm taking you at your word. Here's my address in case you should change your mind while there's still time," and he handed her a card.

She got out of the taxi without saying anything, let herself in, ran to her bedroom, and lying on the bed she cried and cried as she had not done since – since – well, is there any need to go into that? Outside, Mr Spurling pointed out to the leaders of the convoy what very bad dispersion there was in the column.

"What was the v.t.m.?" he asked – but in view of the answer, he decided that the fun was over and he went home.

The next morning he kept an appointment with Mary Sugden while Mrs Lordan-Palfrey made one with the Commissioner of Police.

Mary and Mr Spurling walked in the Park while Mrs Lordan-Palfrey called at Scotland Yard.

"Mary," said Mr Spurling, "I want to warn you against me."

"Why?" said Mary.

"That you will learn quickly enough if you don't take my warning. By the way, I don't want you to take it – but don't say afterwards that I didn't warn you. Helen wouldn't take my warning and now she's miserable."

"What does Helen mean to you?"

"Inasmuch as she introduced me to you, she means a great deal to me."

"What do you mean to her?"

"I'm just a nuisance to her, I assure you. If you ask her, she will warn you against me in even stronger terms than I do. You see, I'm prejudiced in my own favour – so I'm not going too far in persuading you against me. You'll find that Helen is not exactly prejudiced in my favour."

At that moment Mrs Lordan-Palfrey was speaking to the Commissioner in terms which showed how right Mr Spurling was.

"But you, must have some suggestion," she said. "After all, he's had my £12. Surely you can get him six months for that. That would be something."

"It's quite true," said the Commissioner, "that he's had your £12, and if we could prove that we could get him a good deal more than six months. But how can we prove it? He will simply deny it and, unless there is something to show that you must be telling the truth and not he, no prosecution could succeed. It would be far better from your point of view not to have him prosecuted at all than to have him acquitted."

"There must be a law to stop a man forcing £12 out of a woman in a London hotel."

"Oh – very well," sighed the Commissioner. "What I'll do is this. I'll send Hawksley to tax him with the £12 incident and see what he says. If he admits it or says anything we can prove to be a lie we might get him, but I'm not at all hopeful. Let me have his card. I'll send Hawksley straight away and I'll let you know the result of the interview."

"Thank you, Sir Maxwell, I do hope something can be done."

She left Scotland Yard and walked all the way home. It was exactly a week since her first sight of Mr Spurling, but it seemed like a year.

In the Park Mr Spurling was pointing out to Mary that he had known her less than a week. "But I warn you," he said, "I'm after you and your money. I want to be kept in luxury by a lovely and wealthy woman. Don't say I didn't tell you. Before you embark on this adventure, think and think again. I shan't give you another chance. I don't know why I'm giving you this one."

"Anthony," she said, "you're delightful. I'm sure I shall want to buy you soon, if you're still up for sale. Have you ever done anything useful in your life?"

"Only in the war."

"Oh, I don't count that – everyone did something in the war."

"I quite agree. I have no merit at all except a certain degree of frankness – and even that can become annoying."

"How have you lived since the war?"

"As best I could. The only thing I haven't done is to turn to crime. I dare say I should have done if I thought it would have paid. Let's go home and have a drink." They went back to his two-roomed flat off the Edgware Road. They had a drink. In fact they had several. Then the bell rang. He opened the door. Superintendent Hawksley and Inspector Standring came in.

"Mr Spurling?" queried the Superintendent.

"I don't think we've met before," said Mr Spurling.

"My name is Hawksley – and my business is rather confidential. This is Mr Standring. I see you have company. We'll call again."

"No – I must go – really I must," said Mary.

"I'm sorry if we've come at a bad time," said the Superintendent.

"You couldn't have come at a better moment. I should have had another drink if you hadn't. As it is – I shall be able to walk home without assistance. You'll call for me tonight, Tony?"

"Of course."

"No – don't come down."

"You'll break your neck if you go down alone. Excuse me, Mr Hawksley. I'll only be a moment."

They went down the stairs together.

"Are those some of your business friends?" she asked.

"I've never spoken to them in my life," said Mr Spurling, "but I'm sure I know what they want."

"They're not detectives come to arrest you, I suppose?"

"I shouldn't be at all surprised – but they won't stop me from calling for you tonight. Goodbye – darling."

He watched her walk down the street for a moment. Then he returned slowly to the flat.

"Sorry to have kept you," he said.

"I've plenty of time," said the Superintendent. "Now I'll introduce myself properly. You'll understand why I thought it better not to do so before. I'm Superintendent Hawksley of Scotland Yard. This is Inspector Standring."

"Oh yes – what can I do for you?"

"I'm making inquiries into a certain matter and I would like to ask you a few questions."

"By all means. Anything I can do to help."

"I'm not sure that you'll feel like that when you hear the questions. They concern you personally."

"Why not? I have as clear a conscience as most people. Or as little – do I mean? Never mind, please fire away. Cigarette?"

"Thank you, sir. A complaint has been made against you by a lady. We would like to have your version of the story."

"A light?"

"Thank you, sir."

"And the name of the lady?"

"Mrs Lordan-Palfrey."

"Haven't I been taking her out enough, or what?"

"She complains that you have £12 of hers. I would like to know the circumstances in which you obtained it from her."

"She says that I have £12 of hers? That I owe her £12?"

"Precisely."

"She is quite mistaken. There have been some transactions between us, but I can assure you that on balance she is well in my debt – though I shouldn't dream of claiming it."

"Would you give us particulars of the transactions?"

"I'm afraid I can't do that – not unless Mrs Lordan-Palfrey herself asks me to do so. They are quite confidential."

156

"If we obtain a letter of authority from her will that be sufficient?"

"No – I want it from the lady herself. I must be satisfied that she is not being badly advised and that she really wants the whole matter disclosed."

"Would you mind answering this question? Have you at any time been in debt to the extent of £12 to the lady?"

"No – never – not at any time."

"She says you demanded £100 from her with menaces at a hotel and that she handed you £12."

"I have already answered your question. If Mrs Lordan-Palfrey really thinks I owe her any money – which I do not – she is welcome to sue me for it. If she persists in the allegation that I have forced it out of her she is welcome to prosecute me too. I have nothing else to say."

He got up and Scotland Yard got up too.

"I hope I have satisfied you, gentlemen," he said.

"We will report the result of our interview to the Commissioner and we may wish to see you again. I take it you are not proposing to go away."

"Not as far as I know. I will certainly let you know if I change my mind – if you would like me to do so."

"Thank you, sir."

"Don't mention it. Now be careful of the stairs. They're more treacherous going down than coming up."

"We'll never get anything there," said the Superintendent to the Inspector as they drove back.

"I never thought we should. There's much more in it than meets the eye. I'd love to know what those transactions were."

They duly reported to the Commissioner, and he informed Mrs Lordan-Palfrey.

"I've never had any transactions with him. No, I won't see him at any price. I'm finished with the whole affair.

Please write it off your books, or whatever the proper expression is."

The Commissioner telephoned to Charles.

"Thank you for introducing Mrs Lordan-Palfrey, Charles," he said.

"Not at all," said Charles.

"Not at all," said the Commissioner, and hung up the receiver.

Three or four weeks later Miss Mary Sugden completed her purchase and took Mr Spurling for better or for worse. On the same day Mrs Lordan-Palfrey received the following letter from a firm of solicitors:

"On the 10th March last Mr Anthony Spurling handed us £100 to be held by us for you irrevocably on the following terms. You were to pay to him the whole or any part of that sum on demand within six weeks from the date of the deposit. Any balance remaining after the expiry of that period was to become your absolute property. Although the six weeks have not quite expired Mr Spurling informed us yesterday that he will not be making any demands upon you and has instructed us to send you the full amount forthwith. Please acknowledge receipt of the enclosed cheque. Mr Spurling has asked us to convey to you his deep appreciation of the services you have rendered to him and his hope that you were not unduly inconvenienced thereby."

"The tenth of March," she said to herself. "That was the day before we met." Mrs Lordan-Palfrey began to see a little light. The fact that Mr Spurling, by placing £100 to her credit before demanding it, had guarded against the possibility of his being successfully prosecuted did not in the least improve her view of him. Her actual words, when she realised what had happened, surprised even herself, and she required very delicate handling even by her closest admirers for some time afterwards.

In the train taking them on their honeymoon Mr and Mrs Anthony Spurling were talking nonsense. Suddenly she said, "Now I'm really not jealous – but tell me what there was between you and Helen."

"I'll tell you from the start, darling," he said. "I was down and out, the possessor of some wearable clothes and about £200 – unemployed and unemployable. I was desperate. My only hope was to find someone easily deceived, like you, with plenty of money who would keep me and make life possible for me. But how could I find anyone? I did not move in places where you were likely to be found. So I thought of Mrs Lordan-Palfrey. I'd often seen her name in the paper. I went up to her as she was sitting in a London hotel and I said, 'Mrs Lordan-Palfrey – you are famed for your wit, beauty and wisdom. Become famous, too, for your charity.' "

" 'What do you want?' she said.

" 'I am penniless,' I said. 'I must have a rich wife. Introduce me to your friends – be my patroness – and with my natural charm and your introductions I'm sure I can pull it off.'

" 'Certainly,' she said. 'We'll start at once.' "

"Darling, I know Helen; I'm sure it didn't happen like that."

"Well," he conceded, "perhaps not quite like that."

CHAPTER TWELVE

Advertisement

When the Professor had finished he said, "Why – you're still there!"

"Oh, no we're not," said the girl – and a moment later he was alone.

"Now I wonder what Dr Long would say about them," he thought. "I'm certainly no worse than they are."

"Anyway," he said aloud, "this is very, very pleasant."

"I'm so glad you like it," said the proprietor of the hotel, who had just come up behind him.

"Good afternoon," said the Professor. "I thought I was alone – but I certainly meant it. The country round is lovely – this garden is lovely and you run your hotel perfectly."

"It's very kind of you to say so. If I do – it's because I enjoy it. I like to see people happy and comfortable and I can't be happy myself unless they are."

"You should be in the Church," said the Professor.

"I was," said the proprietor, "for a time, but I couldn't make enough headway. I'm too worldly, I suppose. Now this job suits me perfectly, and it's much better paid. Though, honestly, as long as I make sufficient to enable me to live in peace I'm not in the least interested in money. I would always rather charge nothing at all than have a dissatisfied customer. It's quite true that that policy pays in the long run, but that isn't my reason for adopting it."

"I quite believe you," said the Professor. "By the way – am I likely to get a game if I go up to the golf club now?"

"I'll come myself, if you'd like it."

"Very much indeed – if you're not too good," said the Professor.

"I'm very bad," said the proprietor, "but I like the exercise."

They played eighteen holes and returned after tea. The Professor bathed and changed and came down for his glass of sherry.

"Please join me," he said to the proprietor. Over the third glass the latter said, "Please don't think me rude, but weren't you telling a story to the Browns last night?"

"I was."

"I wonder if I could listen to the next one."

"By all means – if there is one," said the Professor. "But I don't yet know if my services will be required."

However, the answer to that question arrived when the Professor was having his dinner, in the shape of a note with one word written on it – "PLEASE." "CERTAINLY," he replied.

He did not expect an answer to that, but it came – "ANGEL."

"I wonder what they'd think at Cambridge," he thought. "I'm sure we'd all be inside if Dr Long had his way."

After dinner they were joined by the proprietor, who took them into his private room. Drinks on the house were provided, and the Professor, feeling in excellent form, told them "Advertisement."

Advertisement

A lovely woman was sitting in the dock at the Old Bailey.
Mr Justice Plank was summing up.

"I will now review the evidence, members of the jury,"
he said. "The accused is the wife of the man with whose
murder she is charged. Until about six weeks before her
husband disappeared she was apparently living with him
on good terms. I say 'apparently,' members of the jury,
because we all know that it is possible for a married couple
to appear happy to others but, in fact, to be very far from
happy. You must exercise your knowledge of the world on
such a matter. As far as the evidence goes, however, there
was no friction between them. About the 9th February last
the husband disappeared and he was never seen again,
unless the corpse, to which I will refer hereafter, is his. His
absence was first noticed by an aunt, who questioned the
accused about him. At that time, of course, there was not
the slightest suspicion of foul play. His aunt simply asked
where he was. The accused replied that he had gone to
Scotland on business. We know now that that was untrue,
or at least highly improbable, because the accused has
quite frankly admitted that she lied. Subsequently, other
inquiries were made by relatives of the missing man and
the accused gave varying explanations for his absence. I
need not detail those explanations, because you heard
them all and the accused has admitted that they were all
false. The accused has told you that her husband and she
agreed to separate for a short time. She has said that she
told lies about his absence because she did not want the
real reason to be known. She asserts that her husband is
still alive, and throughout she has stated, either by herself
or through her counsel, that she is sure her husband will
enter the court before the end of the trial. They had agreed

not to communicate with each other during his absence. As you have heard, the police have made exhaustive inquiries from all hospitals and public institutions in the country to see whether the husband has been admitted to any one of them, ill or injured. The result has been purely negative. That is the evidence, members of the jury. The accused's husband is missing and the accused cannot explain why he does not return in her hour of need. Their separation, she said, was not because they were on bad terms, but simply because they thought it would be a good idea to have a short separation. The present trial has been widely publicised, and you may think that it is, at the least, very improbable that the husband, if alive and in his right mind, would not take some step to bring to the notice of this court that his wife is innocent of the charge. You have probably noticed the accused looking anxiously from time to time to the doors of the court. Was that play acting, members of the jury, or does she really expect her husband to appear? Possibly the remaining evidence in the case will help you to answer that question. You will remember that the witness who first noticed the absence of the accused's husband stated that, although she was not in the least suspicious to begin with, she eventually became so because of a dream. The rules of evidence did not permit her to state what the dream was, but she says that, as a result of it, she asked the police to drag the river. The police have told you that they were at first unwilling to do so, but that subsequently the witness, Mrs Larkins, made a statement to them which changed their minds. Mrs Larkins has made the same statement to you and, although she was considerably cross-examined on the subject, she maintained that what she said was correct. She has told you that on an evening in early February – she cannot give the exact date – she met the accused, who is a neighbour of hers. It was late at night and the accused was assisting a man to carry something heavy out of a car parked by the river. Mrs Larkins could not see the man properly, but she stated that he was the same height as the missing man. She could not see his face. Now a very curious thing happened in this court in regard to that matter. Although the prisoner's counsel had cross-examined Mrs Larkins very severely about the entire incident, the prisoner herself admitted in evidence that it had taken place. She said that the man with her was, in fact, her husband. She refused, however, to state what they were carrying, saying that, if she did so, it might get her husband into trouble. You may think it is straining loyalty too far when a wife, who is liable to be hanged for his murder, refuses to save herself lest she should get him into trouble. However, just in case there might be some deep-laid plot by the husband to kill another man, dress him in his own clothes and then compel his wife to claim the amount due under life policies, I suggested that inquiries should be made from all life insurance companies. As a result of those inquiries it is plain that the husband was not insured at all. You are therefore completely in the dark, members of the jury, as to the crime which the husband was committing that night, and from the consequences of which the accused wishes to shield him. The only person who could have told you has refused to do so. But was it the husband whom she was assisting? Or was the husband merely a corpse which she and her lover were engaged in throwing into the river when seen by Mrs Larkins? The rest of the evidence in the case may help you to solve that problem too. You have heard the evidence that a dead man was recovered from the river. That is not disputed. You have heard also that he was dressed in a suit from which every mark of identity had been removed except a small cleaner's mark which could easily pass unnoticed. You have heard the cleaner swear that the suit belonged to the missing man and that he had cleaned it frequently. He was quite positive on this matter. The accused herself admitted that the suit was exactly like one of her husband's and that they used to employ the cleaner who gave evidence. The body was in too great a state of decomposition to be identified, but the medical evidence showed that the skull had been fractured and that death was due to cerebral haemorrhage, which could have been caused by the injury to the skull. The body was approximately the same size as that of the missing husband. The accused, as you are aware, has absolutely denied that she murdered her husband or had any part in his murder. She says that he is still alive and that the dead man is someone else. On the evidence, as I have so far reviewed it, you might have grave suspicions as to the guilt of the accused, but you might also feel that there was, perhaps, some measure of doubt in the matter. If that were the case the accused is entitled to be acquitted, as I have already told you once and as her counsel has told you at least six times. I come, therefore, to the final piece of evidence in the case, and you must consider whether, in view of that evidence, you feel justified in resolving your doubt against the accused or whether some doubt still remains. A letter was produced by the postmistress of Wardley – a village a few miles from where the accused and her husband lived. This letter was addressed *poste restante* to James Curley, Esq. Mr Curley never called for the letter. It happened that a police inspector was talking to the postmistress and she showed it to him. The inspector took a chance and opened it. It said this: "Darling, I have done it. Come at once." The letter was unsigned, but two handwriting experts have been called by the prosecution and they have both stated that in their opinion the writing is that of the accused. The accused denied that she wrote the letter and the defence called one expert. He said that, although the writing was very similar to that of the accused, it might well have been produced by someone copying from her writing. The prisoner was recalled and asked if she knew of anyone who might conceivably have tried to incriminate her. She said she had no enemies, as far as she knew. The prosecution say that this last piece of evidence clinches the matter. They say that, if the prisoner is innocent, you have got to accept as coincidences the missing husband, the lies by the wife as to his whereabouts, the unexplained and extraordinary incident of the car by the river, the body in the clothes of the husband and finally this letter. Counsel for the defence, on the other hand, says that the accused has sworn that she is innocent. He has invited you, not once but several times, to look at her and ask yourselves whether she seems the sort of woman who would murder her husband. He has, as it were, thrown the appearance of the prisoner into the balance against the weight of the actual evidence. Well, members of the jury, cases are to be tried upon the evidence, but it is, of course, quite right that you should pay close attention to a prisoner's demeanour, particularly in the witness box – though due allowance must be made for his or her natural anxiety. But do you consider that you can read the prisoner's thoughts from her face or figure? If you think you can and you base your verdict upon such imaginings I cannot prevent you, but I am bound to remind you that you have sworn to try the prisoner according to the evidence. The prisoner is undoubtedly a singularly beautiful woman. Do you think it possible that her counsel has seized on that fact to make up for any deficiencies in her defence? It is entirely for you to judge.

I will, indeed, go so far with defending counsel as to agree with him that the prisoner has not either a cruel or degraded face. She certainly has not a face on which is written 'I am a murderess.' But how much that can avail her in view of the evidence it is for you to say. Has everyone who appears in the dock to look like a criminal, and, if he does not, must he be acquitted? I leave such matters and, indeed, the whole of the case to your common sense, members of the jury. I have explained the law to you and you will follow my guidance upon all matters of law. The facts, however, are for you, and if you think I have expressed any opinion on them you will disregard it entirely and form your own. Now, will you please consider your verdict, bearing in mind, as I have said before, that it is not for the prisoner to prove her innocence but for the prosecution to prove her guilt beyond all reasonable doubt."

The jury retired. They returned within half an hour. They found the prisoner guilty. Before she was sentenced to death she was asked whether she had anything to say why sentence should not be passed on her according to law. She said she had. In clear and unfaltering tones she said this: "My Lord, I am innocent of the charge of which I have been convicted and I do not fear the sentence you are about to pronounce. I know that, before it is put into execution, my husband will return and prove me innocent. I would never harm my husband any more than he would harm me. Pronounce the sentence, my Lord. He will ensure that it is never carried out." The Judge pronounced sentence of death, a man in the gallery stroked his beard, and a woman sobbed, but it was not the prisoner.

Twenty years later two prosperous-looking men sat in one of Hubbard's restaurants. They were completing their dinner and a business deal at the same time, and each of them was extremely satisfied with both. It could not have been otherwise with the dinner. Years before, when the first Hubbard restaurant had been opened, a new standard in food had been set. You could dine at Hubbard's, as nowhere else, whether you were a gourmet and very particular, or whether you merely enjoyed good food and good wine and could not distinguish between the good and the exquisite in either. It was not surprising that, three months after the first restaurant had been opened, a second was started, and, not long after that, a third and so on until, some five years after the opening of the first, there were fifty Hubbard restaurants distributed all over the country, each as good as the other and all as good as the first. This was a principle on which John Hubbard had always insisted. He would never open a new restaurant until he had satisfied himself that the employees he had chosen were artistes either in the cooking or service of food, according to their particular positions. He himself was the master and the provision of food and wine was an art in which he was excelled by no one. He considered good eating and drinking to be as important to the human race as good music and good literature and that he had made a substantial contribution to the happiness of his country by opening his fifty restaurants. With the rise in wages after the last war there were comparatively few people who could not afford to go to Hubbard's – at any rate on a special occasion – and the average Englishman and Englishwoman were taught things about food of which they had never dreamed.

One of the two men was, in fact, John Hubbard, and the deal which he was completing was the sale of the entire Hubbard organisation to his friend William Collett. They were not intimate friends, but they were far more than mere business acquaintances. When John and his wife decided to retire they both agreed that they would sell to someone who seemed capable of carrying on the Hubbard tradition. William Collett was such a man. He had not, perhaps, John's genius, but he was deeply interested in the subject and very painstaking and John felt it would be extremely hard to find a more suitable purchaser. William Collett was very keen on the proposition, but he was a businessman and, having seen the figures supplied to him by Hubbard's, he knew the maximum price which he was prepared to pay. John, on the other hand, was quite prepared to sell to the right person for any reasonable amount which would enable him and his family to live in comfort for the rest of their lives. In consequence, as they drank their first glass of port, he accepted a sum which was some £10,000 less than William would have been prepared to pay. They drank a second glass of port to the success of their bargain.

"I knew we shouldn't fall out over the price," said William.

"You've done very well," said John, "but I'm perfectly satisfied, and that's all that matters. The only thing I want now is to complete the whole transaction as soon as possible. How soon can you send in your accountants to vet the books?"

"I shan't send them in at all, old boy. You've given me all the figures. Either they're true or false. I'm prepared to believe they're true. Why should I spend a lot of money just to prove that you're not a liar?"

"Well, it's entirely up to you, Bill. The figures I've given you are, of course, taken from the books and are absolutely correct – but for Heaven's sake don't feel I shall be in the least hurt if you have the books examined. After all, half a million is a lot of money."

"I won't hear another word about it, old boy. We've had deals together before and I know you. I'd even prefer one of us to draft the contract of sale rather than go to solicitors – but we can't go so far as that. My accountants have done very nicely as it is, working out the proper price for me to pay. Pass the port, old boy, please."

They were drinking Cockburn's 1927, of which they still had a few bottles left. It was as good as the '08 had been.

"I'm sure you'll make a great success of it," said John, "because you'll always take the greatest possible interest in the food itself. It means continuous travelling, but, as you like that and always find something new in each part of England you visit, that won't worry you."

"I shall love it. And my wife too. And when we've had enough of it we can always sell out like you. It's twenty years since you began, isn't it?"

"Just on."

"What you must have found quite the hardest part was getting started. Your food can be first class and your service equally so, but unless you have sufficient capital to enable you to pay big rents and indulge in really heavy advertising it's almost impossible to get the public to come before you go bankrupt."

John smiled. "As a matter of fact, I did indulge in really heavy advertising."

"But you told me you hadn't any capital worth speaking of when you started. You surely didn't get credit?"

"No – I certainly didn't get any credit."

"I don't understand it then – or had you a rich uncle?"

"No – I hadn't a rich uncle. As a matter of fact it was a poor, sick tramp who provided the necessary."

"Pass the port, old boy, and repeat that."

"I said it was a poor, sick tramp who enabled us to start."

"A sandwich man, I suppose."

"Not at all. A dead man, shortly after we knew him."

"With an estate in Australia which he left to you, because you befriended him?"

"Not at all – at the end he hadn't even his own clothes."

"I give it up – but it's intriguing. Take some port and tell me."

"If I do tell you, it must be in absolute confidence."

"Of course, old boy, but what's the mystery?"

"Well, if it were known to the police, both my wife and I might get six months."

"This is really interesting. You know I'll keep it to myself. Besides there are no witnesses and you can always say I'm a liar. I am a bit of one anyway. Fire ahead – but just pass the port first."

"All right; now I'm selling the business, I'd rather like to tell someone. You'll be the only person besides Juliet and me who'll know."

"You honour me, old boy."

"I think I do really – but never mind. Let's go and sit in the office. It'll be quieter. Waiter, bring the port to the office, please."

They went to the office and sat down in armchairs. "Come a bit closer," said John. "I don't want to shout."

They arranged themselves and the port satisfactorily, and John began.

"D'you remember the Hubbard murder case about twenty years ago?"

"I can't say I do, off-hand."

"Well, you can take it from me that there was one. My wife was the accused."

"Good Lord! not really? I'm glad she got off."

"She didn't. She was convicted."

"Who was she supposed to have murdered?"

"Me."

William took a quick look at the port and then at John.

"When do I laugh?" he asked.

"Any time you like, but it's perfectly true."

"Don't be silly, old boy. I know we've both had a lot of port, but let's be reasonable. I can see you now and I saw your wife last week. You've both worn remarkably well in the circumstances, I must say."

"Well, if you don't want to hear any more you've only to say so."

"You're not being really serious, old boy, are you?"

"I am."

"But how come, old boy?"

"That's what I'm going to tell you – if you want to hear. It's not the port, I assure you."

"I'm sorry if I sounded a bit incredulous – but you must admit it sounds tall."

"Undoubtedly, but here are the facts as they were presented to the jury at the Old Bailey."

"Then she was really tried?"

"All right, I won't say any more. Have you been to any good shows lately?"

"I'm sorry, old boy, I won't do it again, I promise. Please go on. I believe everything you say. Were you at the Old Bailey? – but, of course not, you couldn't have been."

"As a matter of fact, I was."

"What! Did they bring in the body? But – no, that …," and there William broke off. He was really puzzled. John sipped his port and went on.

"This was the case against my wife."

He then outlined the facts referred to in the summing up of Mr Justice Plank.

"The case aroused very great interest. Most defended murder trials do, and when the accused happens to be a strikingly beautiful woman, with a lovely voice as well, the interest caused cannot fail to be tremendous. My wife's picture, which somehow or other found its way to the press agencies, was published widely, and she had many offers of remarriage – in the event of her acquittal – from admirers who had seen it. I had intended to make a dramatic entry after the Judge's summing up if it were unfavourable, but something about that summing up prompted me not to do so. You will remember that I read for the Bar, although I never practised, and odd passages from the textbooks still stuck in my mind. I had a feeling about that summing up. I also remembered that, before now, a guilty person duly convicted has been acquitted on appeal by reason of a faulty summing up. I could always make my entry in the Appeal Court and I thought it was worth waiting. I notified my wife, through her solicitors, by a previously arranged code what I was going to do, and they passed on the message, not knowing who I was and quite unaware of its meaning. I need hardly tell you that before my disappearance I was clean-shaven. At the trial I had a moustache and beard and hair dyed to the lighter colour of both. Even so, I listened from the gallery and not from the well of the court. In due course the appeal came on for hearing before the Lord Chief Justice and two King's Bench Judges. There I had most forcibly impressed on my mind the principle of English law – that it is better for a hundred guilty men to be acquitted than for one innocent man to be convicted. The case against my wife must have seemed conclusive to any impartial observer. She and I were the only two persons who knew her to be innocent. Yet, in the Court of Criminal Appeal, the three Judges appeared to me to be examining Mr Justice Plank's summing up with a microscope of great power. I will not worry you with the technicalities of the matter. After a day's hearing the court decided that, having regard to some mistakes in the summing up, the conviction could not be upheld and must be quashed. My wife was free and I had not had to do anything. It was what I had hoped for but not expected.

"The day after her acquittal Mrs Hubbard opened the first Hubbard restaurant. All the arrangements had, of course, been made in advance. As she left the Law Courts after her acquittal she had smilingly acknowledged the presence of the numerous reporters and posed for photographs. She granted an interview.

" 'Now I am free,' she said, 'I shall do what my dear husband always wanted to do – open a restaurant. It will be on the Blank by-pass. John had made all the arrangements before we parted. I'm sure he'll come back to me now. You boys have been so good to me during my anxious days that if you can come and have a drink with me on the opening night – tomorrow – I shall be only too pleased.'

"A drink with a really beautiful woman who has been convicted and acquitted of murder was not to be refused, particularly as a good deal of copy could probably be obtained at the same time.

"You don't, of course, remember the first days at our restaurant. I had been ready and was not taken unawares. I had risked everything and had supplies for thousands – and thousands came. They came in the first instance to look at my wife's lovely neck and to visualise what might have happened to it. But they were given food which many of them had never tasted before. You know now what I can do. I spent everything we had on making sure that everything would be superb; and superb it was. It was summertime and we were really lucky in the weather. We filled the garden with tables – every room was filled with tables – and yet, once you sat down to your meal, it was as it is today – no waiting – yet no flurry – everything perfect. I had engaged hundreds of waiters for the first night and erected special emergency kitchens.

"After about a fortnight I appeared myself – in my beard, of course. I came as manager. My name was John Brown. Everyone believed that I was really James Curley and the police even interviewed me. I knew my rights, however, and, beyond telling them I was not and never had been James Curley, I said nothing at all. They no doubt said a good deal to themselves, but they could do nothing about it. The rumour that James Curley was also on view – although the law of libel prevented it from being mentioned in the papers – quickly spread, and people came down to see me as well. Gradually, however, the interest in us as a pair of murderers died down, but the interest in our food did not. We were made from the first day and have never looked back. Perhaps you'll agree now that we went in for big advertising."

"Yes, old boy, but what about the body?"

"It was the body which gave me the whole idea. A tramp came begging to our house. He was obviously very ill – my wife and I were very much in love and our natural sympathy was even stronger than usual at the time. We took him in, made him as comfortable as possible and sent for our doctor. He told us it was a hopeless case and that the man had better go to the infirmary. We refused – and I really believe that that man's last few days were some of the happiest he had had. He literally cried for joy. He had probably never experienced such kindness before. It was no credit to us. We just felt we had to. We did all we could for him, but he died shortly afterwards of cerebral haemorrhage. The doctor gave me a certificate, and it was while I was on my way to the registrar that the idea gradually came to me. My wife and I had a lease of a house on the Blank by-pass and between £1,000 and £2,000. I had no job and did not seem likely to get a congenial one or one at which I could make a success. We had decided to turn our house into a restaurant. I had always had this flair for food, and my wife was a very capable cook and able to teach others. As I've told you before – you don't need the highest-paid chefs to run a good restaurant. All you require is really good food, really good recipes, a man like myself and a capable cook. I'll guarantee that there are thousands of men and women who, after a little training, could prepare the excellent dinner we had tonight. Well – our trouble was lack of capital.

"So many places had failed for that reason, and, although we knew our food would be exceptional, we couldn't afford to advertise to any great extent. To acquire a reputation in such circumstances would take a very long time. So, before committing ourselves, we tried to think of some publicity stunt we could produce to give the place a good start. On the way to the registrar I thought of this one. You'll say it was a mad idea – so it was, but we were prepared to take the risk. I could at any moment have proved who the dead man was and that I'd registered his death and that I was alive. The doctor's certificate proved that the man died of natural causes. So there was no chance of my wife or me being hanged. Naturally I made provision for the possibility of my dying before the trial.

"If everything had gone wrong and our conspiracy was brought to light, we could only have been given a short term of imprisonment for creating a public mischief and disposing of a dead body. We naturally didn't want that, but we were adventurers and very ambitious. Accordingly, as soon as I'd registered the death I talked to Juliet about my idea. As you know, she has great determination and I judged her capable of going through with it. She agreed. We put the tramp in a suit of mine on which we left only the cleaner's mark. I gave the skull a bit of a crack and then we threw him in the river.

Unfortunately, we met Mrs Larkins on the way. I hadn't intended that piece of evidence, as it weighted the case too much against Juliet. However, I managed not to show my face and we decided to carry on. The letter was written by me, imitating Juliet's handwriting. I did this so that she need not commit perjury in the witness box. Had the police inspector not happened to come upon it we should have put him on the scent anonymously. The rest you know – except that in due course we pretended to get married and I changed my name to Hubbard. Five years ago, you'll remember, I shaved off my beard and moustache. And that is the story behind Hubbard's restaurants."

William hesitated a moment or two before he made any comment. Then – "Very interesting," he said. "You won't think it offensive of me, old boy, will you, if I send in my accountants to look at your books after all?"

CHAPTER THIRTEEN

Music for All

"I hope," said the proprietor, when the Professor had finished, "that your complimentary references to this hotel are not also intended to suggest that I started in much the same way as Mr Hubbard."

"Oh dear, no," said the Professor. "To begin with you're not married, as far as I know."

"That is true," said the proprietor, "nor am I unscrupulous."

"Perhaps you will remedy the first distinction one of these days."

"That may well be," was the reply. "Each of those young ladies who wait on you at meals is, I believe, a candidate for my affections. I have told them all that I am not likely to fall for any of them in that way, but apparently they live in hopes. In any event, they are excellent waitresses and play quite a reasonable game of tennis. That's funny. I didn't notice Mr and Mrs Brown slip away."

"I should have explained," said the Professor, "at least, perhaps I should not. However, I can assure you that they did not mean to be rude. I think, now, that I will follow their excellent example and say good night."

"Good night, Mr Mowbray," said the proprietor. "Just look at the moon," he added as he opened the door for the Professor. "It's almost bright enough to play tennis. I rather feel like a game."

"A curious time for tennis," said the Professor.

"Oh, I don't know," said the proprietor, and they went their respective ways.

And so the days went on, pleasantly enough for the Professor. He played golf or took some other form of exercise during the day, enjoyed his excellent meals and took a great liking for his new companions. One evening at dinner he received a note from the usual source which read as follows: "WE HAVE WRITTEN A STORY."

He replied, "I LOOK FORWARD TO HEARING IT."

Answer came back, "IT IS VERY SHORT."

"WHAT A PITY," he wrote.

"WAIT TILL YOU'VE HEARD IT," they replied.

In due course he joined them in the lounge and they went to their usual corner.

"I hope you won't be disappointed in it," said Mrs Brown.

"I'm sure I shan't be."

"But please say what you really think. You will, won't you?"

"All right," said the Professor with a smile, "but why you should be apprehensive after listening to mine I can't think."

"It's so different," said Mrs Brown.

"That will be an advantage, I have no doubt," said the Professor. "Which of you will read it?"

"George is going to – aren't you, darling?" said Mrs Brown.

"Oh, very well," said George. "Here it is," and he read "Music for All."

Music For All

Vivian Stammers was deeply interested in music. He played little himself but he had a considerable knowledge of the subject and derived intense enjoyment from listening. He was not a professional musician – indeed, he was a stockbroker – but he could hold his own in technical discussions with any member of the profession.

So devoted was he to music that he rarely mixed with men or women who were not at least fond of it too. If he met a girl at a dance for the first time and in reply to his early question "Do you like music?" she answered, as many did, "Oh – passionately – I adore opera," that was the end as far as Vivian was concerned. The only reply real music lovers would give to Vivian's question was, "Yes, I do," or, "Yes, very much indeed." They would not dream of giving a reason for the answer, least of all opera. So, many aspiring mothers – for Vivian's stock as a bachelor stood high in the marriage market – saw their hopes dashed to the ground through taking their daughters, the day before they met him, to "Tosca" or "Madame Butterfly."

Vivian's friends were accordingly most surprised when he eventually married a wealthy but charming girl who did not even love opera. Mary Lutterworth had no knowledge of music whatever and, until she married Vivian, she had no wish to acquire such knowledge. She could not have distinguished one symphony of Beethoven from another, nor could she have told the difference between the music of Brahms and Mozart. Although his friends were surprised, they soon realised that Vivian had been no fool in choosing Mary. She was attractive to look upon, she had a sweet voice and delightful manners; but her great value as a wife was her extreme selflessness and loyalty. Usually it is uncomplimentary to call a person kind, but Mary's kindness had such depths that it was remarkable. She could not bear to see anyone suffer, least of all the man to whom she was married. Accordingly, her life's work from the time she married Vivian was to do all in her power to make him happy, at whatever cost to herself. Fortunately, she was also quite intelligent and she was careful not to overwhelm him with stupid attentions, which, bearable or even amusing on a honeymoon, would become intolerable as a daily occurrence. It was perhaps, therefore, not so strange that he should marry her when he realised her qualities. It was strange, however, that he ever got to know her, having regard to his behaviour towards girls who knew nothing of music. In fact, it was due to an accident. He met her at a dance and, as usual, said, "Do you like music?" She misheard him and thought he said "the music" and was referring to the dance band, which was excellent. She answered, obviously with enthusiasm, "Yes, very much." By chance they found so many other subjects to discuss that he had become interested in her before he knew of the mistake.

After that, it was not long before Vivian decided that one musical member of the family would be quite enough. So he married her and for a time they lived very happily. Her ignorance of music was treated by Vivian and his friends as a stock joke. When they came round in the evening and had reached a late stage in their discussion on some musical topic, Vivian would turn playfully to Mary and ask for her opinion. She never appeared to be hurt nor would she have admitted to herself that she was. After some time, however, the joke began to pall and Vivian to feel irritated that his wife could not understand the language he spoke so often and that it was useless to talk to her in it. She saw the irritation and tried her hardest to prevent it. But it was no good. He would for instance see in *The Times* that their musical critic had precisely the same comment to make on a piece of phrasing by Toscanini in the concert the night before as he had made himself during the interval at the concert. What was the good of telling Mary? He knew that it really meant nothing to her.

He began to say he would be late back from the office and to go out with his friends. Mary suffered in silence and never showed him that she knew. Then one day when she was buying some records for Vivian, the pleasant young assistant, who always served her, said quite unexpectedly, "Why do you buy all these records, Mrs Stammers? You don't like music yourself."

"They're for my husband."

"What a pity you don't enjoy them too."

"Yes, isn't it?"

"You could, you know."

"I could?"

"Certainly, if you took a little trouble over it, provided, of course, that you're not tone deaf."

"I'm certainly not tone deaf."

"You like a good tune?"

"Very much."

"Then why not try?"

"How do I start?"

"I'll show you, if you've a moment now."

"I have indeed."

Mary's heart was beating fast. If this young man could really show her how to appreciate good music everything would be all right again. I wonder how long it will take, she thought. Shall I tell Vivian or wait and surprise him? I wonder if I'll really be able to do it. All this and more she thought during the ten seconds it took the assistant, Mr

Willoughby, to lead her into one of the cubicles where customers tried out records.

"Now, the first thing I want you to realise," he said, "is that in classical music you will find some of the most beautiful tunes in the world. But the untrained ear is at first unable to detect many of them. It is true that in some music, such as some of Mozart's violin sonatas, the music is so simple and the tune so lovely that anyone, even you, now, could pick it out at the first time of hearing. In most of Beethoven, however, the tune does not lie so easily on the surface. Consequently, the man or woman who is already frightened of what is called highbrow music never has a chance to hear it. So the first lesson is – listen for the tune. I will help you find it. Now, are you sure that I'm not being just a nuisance? I'd hate to be."

"On the contrary, it's I who am going to be the nuisance, if you can really help me."

"I'm only too pleased. You will find that it becomes easier and easier to pick out the tune as your ear becomes accustomed to doing so. Eventually, you will have no difficulty at all, even with quite difficult composers."

So she spent an hour trying to learn to like music. She thanked Mr Willoughby very much and made an appointment for another lesson. She did not feel she had got very far, but his last words to her had been, "Now, do trust me. I know what I'm talking about. I'll guarantee that if you come again seven times you will be well on the road to success." So she went home with some hope, but by no means convinced. Mr Willoughby on the other hand was very pleased with himself. It looked as though she really would come again and it was not often that he could enjoy an hour alone with a woman as charming as Mary Stammers.

Mary decided to say nothing at all to Vivian. In the first

place it might be a failure, and secondly, it would be far more effective if she could go to him one day and show that she had at last entered into his world. So she went ahead with her lessons and, to her amazement, what Mr Willoughby had said turned out to be true. After seven appointments she could really pick out the main tunes in all the movements of the "Eroica." Little by little he took her from piece to piece and from composer to composer until even much of Bach became a joy to her.

After about the fourteenth lesson she said to Mr Willoughby, "You know, I ought to be paying you for this – but it's really worth so much more to me than I can tell you that I can't think of anything to offer."

"That's perfectly all right," he said. "I'm paid by the firm. It encourages business. You as well as your husband will be customers in the future. It's what I'm here for."

"Yes, but you're doing far more for me than for your other customers. Why, you may even be losing business for yourself while you're sitting here with me."

"Well, if you insist on paying me – "

"I would very much like to."

"Well – I would rather like a kiss."

Mary coloured. "Please don't be silly," she said.

"I'm sorry. I really am terribly sorry, but I was tempted. Please forget it."

"Of course. I'm not in the least annoyed. It's quite a compliment, really. Now let's get on."

So they went on, week after week, until Mary not merely acquired a considerable knowledge of op. numbers but a very genuine love for the music itself. She also found it a refreshing change to be receiving instead of always giving. Finally there came the day when she could appreciate Bach's "Art of Fugue." That took quite a long time, but not as long as Mr Willoughby would have liked.

MUSIC FOR ALL

It was at that stage that Mary decided she knew enough to break it to Vivian. She was very excited. She had so often been miserable at the thought of Vivian's loneliness – for that is what she felt it amounted to – that tears came into her eyes as she imagined his joy at finding that she was a new being. His suffering would be over and she could not bear to see anyone suffer. She decided to bring him a large quantity of records and gradually to display her knowledge as she discussed them with him. How amazed he would be when he heard her say, "I think the third Rasoumovsky is far the best," even if he disagreed, or even if he disliked any quartet of Beethoven being referred to as the best.

After breakfast on the great day she said to Vivian, "Will you try and make a point of being home early tonight, darling?"

"Oh? Yes, certainly. But why?"

"You'll see when you come."

He kept his word and was back early, but he did not seem in the least inquisitive as to why she had asked him. Before she mentioned the subject he said, rather awkwardly, "Darling, I'm rather glad I've come home early – I wanted to have a chat with you."

"Yes, of course, but won't it wait for a few minutes? I've got something for you." She produced the parcels – she had made a selection which gave her the best opportunity of showing off her knowledge.

"I've got a few records, darling. We haven't had many recently. Here's a new recording of Haydn's 'Joke' quartet. It's very good."

"What do you know about the 'Joke' quartet?"

"Oh – I like it. It's a very good joke too."

"I didn't know you'd even heard of it."

"Oh, I've heard of quite a lot in the last few months."

185

"You seem to – if all these volumes are any criterion. But I'm afraid you've got to hear of something more – and it's very unpleasant. I want you to divorce me. I want to marry Anne Crockford."

"Anne Crockford? She plays beautifully."

"I didn't know you'd heard her."

"Oh, on records, you know. Yes, there's a new recording of her doing the Emperor Concerto."

"I dare say," he said rather roughly, "but what about it?"

"Oh! darling," she said. "If you want to – that's all there is to it."

Mary was, indeed, a woman in a thousand or ten thousand. In spite of all its implications she had given no sign that his statement had been of any more importance to her than the suggestion of a visit to the theatre.

"Well, you'll divorce me, then?"

"Yes, certainly, darling, but not before dinner." Vivian was much relieved and ate a larger dinner than he had eaten for days. He had been really worried.

After the meal she put on a Brandenburg concerto and, when it was over, told him what she'd been doing. He was delighted. "Think what you've been missing. You'll be able to make up for lost time now."

The next day Mary went to see Mr Willoughby at the shop. She had promised to let him know how it went off.

"I'd like to hear one of Anne Crockford's new recordings – there's a Beethoven Sonata, isn't there?"

"Yes, I'll get it." He fetched the sonata and they entered a cubicle. "Well," he said, "how did it go?"

"Better than I could possibly have expected, my darling," she said.

CHAPTER FOURTEEN

In Broad Daylight

"Thank you very much," said the Professor. "Unfortunately I am tone deaf or I should certainly try out Mr Willoughby's theory myself. I am sure I must be missing a great deal. Now do you wish to be bored for a little or have you had enough of me tonight?"

Mr and Mrs Brown looked at each other.

"We should like a short one, please," said Mrs Brown.

"Well, as you can always leave in the middle the length doesn't really matter much, does it? By the way, what is the date?"

"The seventeenth."

"Let me see," said the Professor, "that gives me another four days."

"How curious," said Mr Brown. "We're leaving then too. May I ask where you're going to?"

"To Cambridge, probably."

"How extraordinary. We live in Soham – that is, we're just going to. George is a doctor and he's gone into partnership there."

"Well," said the Professor, "if, when you're a staid married couple of three months' standing, your views about Professors of law haven't undergone a change, I shall look forward to seeing you."

"I didn't know you taught there, Mr Mowbray – or it should be Professor Mowbray, I suppose?"

"Oh!" said the Professor, "I shouldn't have told you that. Let me think for a moment."

He remained silent for a minute, thinking hard. Dr and Mrs Brown looked puzzled. Finally the Professor said, "I'm sure you will treat what I say confidentially."

"Oh, of course," they answered.

"Well, I can't tell you everything now, but I'm not travelling under my own name, and I don't want it to be known that I am a Professor of law – or indeed a Professor of anything at all. I'll tell you why one day. At the moment I can only assure you that I'm not a fugitive from justice."

"You certainly don't look like one," said Mrs Brown. "Though it would be very exciting if you were."

"Well, I must disappoint you there," said the Professor, "although I admit that my little holiday has not been without excitement."

At that moment the local inspector of police in uniform entered the lounge.

"I want to see the proprietor," he said to the waitress. She showed him out of the lounge to the office.

"Do you want to hide?" said Mrs Brown to the Professor.

It was an awkward question, because he certainly did want to hide. However, he felt it would be unwise to give himself away so soon. The Inspector's visit was probably nothing to do with him. At the same time – and, at the thought of Tapworth House and Dr Long and the domineering Sisters, the Professor started to break into a cold sweat. He pulled himself together. "This won't do," he decided.

"No – I don't think I'll hide, yet," he said. "Not until I've finished the story anyway. Are you ready?"

"We are all attention," said Mrs Brown, and the Professor told them "In Broad Daylight."

In Broad Daylight

We were bemoaning the fate of George. He had just gone down for another eighteen months and he'd been out only three months from his last stretch.

"He was too ambitious," said Tiny. "Trying to take away half the contents of a house."

"The owner was away," said George's pal, who had not been caught.

"Yes," agreed Tiny, "but carting furniture away in broad daylight is asking for trouble."

"I don't know about that," said Mr Parker. He had only recently been introduced to us. "I have done it myself and even got the police to help. In Park Lane, too. Would you care to hear about it?" We said we would.

"You remember," he said, "just before the beginning of the war a number of wealthy people suddenly found they had important business in America or New Zealand, shut up their houses and went off like a streak of lightning."

We remembered.

"Well, I thought I'd call on one of them just to see if everything was going on all right in his absence. I noticed a nice house in Park Lane with shutters up. I looked for the house in a directory and found that Mr Alfred Poppleton lived there. I decided to see how Mr Alfred Poppleton's affairs were going on. I called one afternoon. I rang the bell in case there was a caretaker. There was – in the person of a toothless old hag with an impediment in her speech and considerable impediments in her intelligence. However, I did manage to find out from her that Mr Poppleton was in America and that any

189

communication for him should be sent to his Bank – Barclays or Lloyds, I forget which. I also was able to see that the house had been left fully furnished – and in very good taste too, I may say. I managed to persuade the hag to show me over. I decided I would like Mr Poppleton's furniture. After all, if he'd really been attached to it he shouldn't have left it behind like that. Before I went, I told the hag that Mr Poppleton owed me a lot of money, but I don't know if she took it in. I then consulted Messrs Hogg and Cooper, a very respectable firm of solicitors, and I told them that Mr Alfred Poppleton of No. 180 Park Lane owed me £10,000. Would they try to recover it for me? I told them the circumstances in which the money came to be owed and I produced an odd letter or two in which Mr Poppleton had promised to pay me as soon as he could. I gave Messrs Hogg and Cooper £10 in cash on account of costs and asked them to proceed as speedily as possible. Mr Cowley, their managing clerk, was delighted. Claims for £10,000 were not too common and, anyway, if it turned out to be nonsense £10 on account of costs would keep Messrs Hogg and Cooper on the right side. I gave them my name (or rather the name under which I was then working) and my address. I'd taken a flat for a week or so. I also mentioned casually that Mr Poppleton was staying down at a hotel in Surrey – the Grantley Arms Hotel, Sibley – in case of air raids, I added. I left Mr Cowley beaming, and I took the next train down to Sibley. I put up at the Grantley Arms Hotel under the name of Alfred Poppleton.

A few days later I found a letter in my rack. It was from Messrs Hogg and Cooper. It said that they had been consulted by Mr Raymond Aspinall of 10 Bar Court in regard to a sum of £10,000 which I owed him. Their client had acted with great patience but could not wait for his money any longer. Would I please send them a cheque for that amount together with 13s 4d (their costs), or alternatively the name of a solicitor who would accept service of proceedings on my behalf. An impudent claim, I said to myself, and with the letter in my pocket I went straight to that highly reputable firm of solicitors, Messrs Reeve and Ruddick.

"I am Alfred Poppleton of 180 Park Lane," I said to the managing clerk who interviewed me.

"Please sit down," he said. "Mr Reeve will see you." Shortly afterwards I was shown in to Mr Reeve's office.

"Good morning, sir," he said. "Do you mind telling me on whose introduction you are consulting us?"

"*The Evening News*," I said. "I was struck by the way you handled that claim against Sir George Martin. I have an equally impudent claim against me, but for twice as much, and I rather suspect the same people are behind the plaintiff."

"Most interesting," said Mr Reeve. "Perhaps you will tell me all about it."

I produced the letter from Messrs Hogg and Cooper.

"I know Hogg and Cooper," I said, "and I'm quite sure they wouldn't put forward what they know to be a false claim, but their client is lying to them. Personally I think it is merely bluff. I don't owe the man a penny and, if you write back a strong letter, I think he'll drop the whole thing. If he carries his bluff as far as a writ by all means accept service on my behalf. No doubt you would like me to give you a retainer."

"I will have one prepared," said Mr Reeve, and rang the bell.

"If you want to get in touch with me I am staying at the moment at the Grantley Arms Hotel, Sibley. I've shut up my house. Not that I'm frightened of bombing for myself – but it's not fair on the servants. As you don't know me,"

I added, "perhaps you'd like something on account," and I handed him what I called the nominal sum of £10. I duly signed the retainer and took leave of an extremely polite Mr Reeve. Two days later, while I was staying at Bar Court, a letter arrived from Messrs Hogg and Cooper asking me to call. I called. I was shown a letter from Messrs Reeve and Ruddick. It stated that they and their client were amazed at the impudent claim put forward by Mr Aspinall and added they would be pleased to accept service of a writ if proceedings were seriously intended, which, they added, they took leave to doubt.

"Very well," I said, "go right ahead. I'll give him 'impudent claim.' Can the writ be served on him personally?" I added.

"Quite impossible, I'm afraid," said Mr Cowley. "Contrary to professional etiquette. His solicitors have agreed to accept service."

"But he deserves it," I said. "I'd like to serve him in the presence of his bankers."

"I'm afraid we couldn't possibly do that, sir."

"Oh, well," I said regretfully, "it can't be helped – but sue him at once and make the costs as heavy as possible."

Mr Cowley smiled. "We'll certainly do our best."

"Meanwhile," I said, "I imagine you will like a little more on account," and I handed him £20. Mr Cowley gave me a receipt and I left for Sibley. Sure enough, a few days later I received a letter from Messrs Reeve and Ruddick stating that Mr Aspinall had issued a writ and they had accepted service on my behalf. Would I call at my convenience to discuss the conduct of the case, the briefing of counsel, etc.? I duly called.

"Tell me, Mr Reeve," I said, "how long can I keep the plaintiff out of his money without spending more than

£20 on my own costs?"

Mr Reeve was a little surprised. "Do you mean you owe the money?" he asked.

"Well," I said, "it's a long story and, on consideration, I don't feel inclined to go into court about it. But if I can keep the plaintiff off for a week or two, he'll have to whistle for his money anyway."

"That can be done quite easily."

"Very well, then," I said. "Hold him off for three weeks and then consent to judgment. Don't ask me where I'm going or what I'm going to do. Just tell me how much you want for your own costs to carry out those instructions."

Mr Reeve rang a bell and consulted his costs clerk. He would require a further £15. I produced the cash.

"Can you assure me," I said, "that judgment will not be obtained against me for three weeks?"

"I can," said Mr Reeve.

"Very well," I said. " Is there anything more you require of me?"

"No, thank you," said Mr Reeve.

"Well, good morning, then," I said, "and thank you very much for your help. I don't suppose you will ever see me again and certainly Mr Aspinall won't."

And with that I departed and gave up my room at the Grantley Arms Hotel. In due course – three weeks later to be exact – I was again asked to call on Messrs Hogg and Cooper.

"Good news, Mr Aspinall," said Mr Cowley, though he didn't look terribly pleased, "the defendant has submitted to judgment."

"Good," I said. "Can I have a cheque?"

"Oh! he hasn't paid yet."

"But he must," I said, "and at once. He'll do me out of it if he can. He'll do a bunk and take everything away with him. What can you do to stop him?"

"Well," said Mr Cowley, "if he doesn't pay at once we could put in execution at his house – that is, if he has anything there."

"Anything there!" I said. "It's full of stuff. At least it was," I added anxiously. "You'd better hurry."

"I'll ring up his solicitors and ask what proposals their client has for satisfying the judgment."

He did so. He talked to Mr Reeve. Eventually he put down the receiver.

"I believe you're right," he said. "From what Reeve told me I think he's withdrawn his instructions from them and is going to make off."

"What can you do?" I said.

"I'll put the sheriff in as quickly as possible," said Mr Cowley. "We have leave to enforce the judgment."

"Good," I said. "Will you need me any more?"

"No, thank you, except just to sign this authority. Thank you. You can rely on my getting on with it at once."

Three weeks later I watched with interest the removal of all the furniture from 180 Park Lane. As each pantechnicon was ready a policeman held up the traffic to let it out. From what I could see the toothless hag did not seem unduly worried. Shortly afterwards I received a cheque from Messrs Hogg and Cooper for £7,500. They were sorry the furniture did not fetch enough to satisfy the entire judgment, but, after deducting the sheriff's costs and charges and their own costs, that was all that was left. Would I send my instructions as to the recovery of the balance?

I cashed the cheque for £7,500 and wrote to Messrs Hogg and Cooper that I was very disappointed at the amount recovered and that I would not trouble them any more. And I didn't.

CHAPTER FIFTEEN

On Appeal

"Could that really be done?" said Mrs Brown.

"It's quite possible," said the Professor, "though, of course, if the owner were communicated with in time the sale would be held up and the scheme discovered. However, at that stage of the war the flight of some people was so precipitate that they might easily have failed to make satisfactory arrangements for such communication. But I see the proprietor and Inspector coming towards us. I wonder what they want."

There was no means of escape and the Professor decided to put a bold face on it. There were four days to go – and somehow or other he had got to get through them.

"Can we trouble you a moment?" said the proprietor. "All of us," said the Professor, "or only me?"

"Just you, Mr Mowbray, thank you," said the proprietor.

"It looks bad," said Mrs Brown. "We'll come and see you in prison – if you're allowed visitors. Good night – and good luck." Dr and Mrs Brown withdrew.

"This is Inspector Martin," said the proprietor.

"How d'you do?" said the Professor. "In what way can I help you? Please sit down."

They sat down next to the Professor. The Inspector was a burly man. Much stronger than I am, thought the Professor, and I never could run fast.

"Yes, Inspector?" he said.

"I understand from Mr Bennett here" (and the Inspector indicated the proprietor) "that you arrived here by the 4.30 train on the eighth. Is that right?"

"I dare say," said the Professor. "I haven't a very good head for dates or times, but it was about that date and about that time."

"Mr Bennett tells me quite definitely that it was," said the Inspector. "He has, of course, his record of the date."

"No doubt, no doubt," said the Professor. "But you won't think me rude if I ask you to come to the point. I am, of course, only too pleased to help you in any inquiries you may be making, but I cannot think what assistance I can give, and, to be quite candid, it's past my bedtime. You wouldn't care to come tomorrow, I suppose?" he added hopefully.

"Quite impossible, I'm afraid," said the Inspector.

"Then what is it I can do for you?"

The Inspector took out his notebook.

"May I have your full name and address, please, sir?" he said.

"Has Mr Bennett not given them to you, Inspector?" said the Professor a little sharply. "I really don't understand this procedure. What is it you want?"

"I'm sorry to have annoyed you, sir," said the Inspector, "but, whenever I take a statement, I take the name and address of the maker first."

"Well, you know mine. Why ask me for it?"

"I've only a name, I'm afraid," said the Inspector. "Mr James Mowbray."

196

"Very well," said the Professor, "my present address is 16 Danes Court, Knightsbridge, London. Are you going to caution me that anything I say may be used in evidence?"

"Oh – dear no – sir," said the Inspector, "and I'm extremely sorry to have disturbed you at this time of night."

That sounds all right, thought the Professor, and relaxed a little.

"I'm afraid I can't help myself in my job," went on the Inspector. "Messages come in at all times of the day and night. Only as I was leaving the office tonight I had a wire about an escaped lunatic."

"Indeed," said the Professor, "this is all very interesting, but how am I expected to help you in the matter?" He was amazed at the calm way in which he asked the question. He hoped they could not hear how fast his heart was beating.

"Oh – it's not about him, sir," said the Inspector. "It's about the train you took. Do you happen to remember whether it stopped at Boreham Halt?"

"I haven't the faintest idea," said the Professor.

"Would you try and think, sir? There was a theft of baggage during the journey and some of the goods have been found near there. Now the guard and driver say the train never stopped, but one of the passengers says he is quite sure that it did. We've no reason to suspect the guard or the driver, but we have to check up on their story."

"I'm afraid I haven't the remotest idea," said the Professor happily. "I was probably asleep."

"Well, I'm sorry to have troubled you, sir," said the Inspector, and rose to go.

"Not at all," said the Professor very pleasantly. "You have your duty to do. I'm sorry if I seemed abrupt – but I'm a little tired. By the way – just to prevent your coming in the middle of the night and asking me about the escaped lunatic, perhaps you'd ask me now."

"I'm afraid you can't help there, sir. It was just a wire to tell us that a man, who escaped some ten days ago, is still at large. They send them to all police stations in the country. From the original notification we had I expect he's in Scotland in fact, but we have to keep our eyes and ears open."

"Quite so," said the Professor. "I confess I shouldn't like to find one crawling into my bedroom."

"Oh – this one is quite harmless. Escaped from near Cambridge and was thought to be making for Scotland. Has a curious form of mania. Telling stories."

"Telling stories?" said the proprietor, and looked at the Professor.

"That seems harmless enough," said the Professor, stifling a yawn. "I tell quite a lot myself. Well – good night, gentlemen," and he got up and went slowly out of the lounge.

While undressing, he considered what would be his best course of action. Did the hotel proprietor suspect anything? And, if he did, would he tell the Inspector? There was no clear answer to either question. If he left, would it excite suspicion? If he stayed, how much risk would he run? Again there was no clear answer. He decided to sleep on it. But he couldn't. After an hour or so of restlessness he turned on the light and picked up a magazine. In it he read "On Appeal."

On Appeal

The butler told me that nothing had been touched, and I found Mr Justice Kingsdown – or rather his body – sitting in a chair. There was a bullet wound in the head and a revolver lay close beside. Careful investigation showed quite clearly that it was suicide. But why? Why had one of our most eminent Judges taken his life? At first, there seemed no clue at all, unless the newspaper he must have been reading just before his death could be considered one. He had apparently been looking at the report of an appeal in the Court of Criminal Appeal. It was an appeal from a conviction in a case he had tried, but I could not conceive how that could have anything to do with it. In point of fact, it was seldom indeed that any decision of his was interfered with or any summing up of his in a criminal case adversely commented on. He was the leading criminal Judge, fair to a degree but stern and unbending and a terror to the guilty. Many a criminal I have known has decided to plead guilty rather than face a trial before him. Of course, every Judge makes mistakes sometimes. Even the Court of Criminal Appeal, which is ordinarily the supreme court in criminal matters, makes mistakes. But I could not think that, even had his conduct of the case been criticised, such a matter could have any connection with his suicide.

Shortly afterwards, however, I had a clue – a most unpleasant one. The Judge's little daughter was found dead – murdered – in a wood. The medical evidence showed conclusively that she must have died a day before her father. The public immediately assumed the worst – that for some reason the Judge had killed his daughter and then committed suicide. But this did not make sense to me. There was overwhelming evidence that he doted on his daughter. He was a widower and she was his only child and it was plain that his whole private life centred round the little girl. If there had been some evidence that he had gone mad the matter would have been different, but, right up to the moment of his death, he had been quite normal.

I told my chief at the Yard that I was not satisfied with the generally accepted explanation and that I was going to make further inquiries. And I made them. Some weeks later, partly by hard work and partly by luck, I had solved the mystery and, though this could not bring the dead back to life, I was glad to be able to clear the good name of Mr Justice Kingsdown. I had appeared as a witness before him in quite a number of cases and I had always liked and admired him. Moreover, several times he had commended me for my work, and even a Superintendent of the CID is not averse to this. I will not trouble you with the details of my investigation. I will simply tell you what I discovered.

My refusal to believe that the Judge could have been a party to his daughter's murder was fully borne out by the results of my inquiries. It was, indeed, his overwhelming attachment to her which led to his death. She used to go with him frequently to Assizes and it was while he was on circuit that the tragedy began to take shape. During a short stroll by himself one night before dinner the Judge was suddenly accosted by a stranger, who asked him if he could spare a few minutes.

"For what purpose?" asked the Judge.

"I wanted to speak to you about the Shepherd case you are trying tomorrow," was the reply.

"That is quite impossible."

"But, please, try to make it possible, sir," begged the stranger. "I am the father of the accused."

"I'm sorry," said the Judge. "I cannot in any circumstances discuss the matter with you. Good evening."

"But I must speak to you. It's terribly important. He mustn't hang. I couldn't bear it."

"Your son will be tried, I hope, fairly – and there is nothing more I can say to you," and the Judge walked away.

But Shepherd's father was persistent, and walked with him. "You will have to listen to me," he said, "and when I tell you that your daughter's safety is concerned – "

He did not finish the sentence, nor was there any need.

The Judge stopped at once.

"What do you mean?" he said.

"Just this," said the man. "Your daughter no doubt means everything to you. My son means everything to me. On the day my son is convicted he will be a dead man to me – and your daughter will be dead to you too."

"Are you mad?" said the Judge.

"Possibly, but quite determined. I know my son has a difficult case. I know he's very likely to be convicted. I know, too, that, if he is convicted, no Home Secretary would dream of granting a reprieve. I don't care how guilty he is. I want him to live – and there's only one way of making sure that he does. You're the only person who can save him. Lend the jury a hand and they'll let him off."

"I shall do nothing of the sort."

"Then you will lose your daughter."

"I will take precautions about that, and I warn you that I shall report this matter to the police immediately."

"I shouldn't if I were you, and even if you do, you're a bit late. I'm afraid you won't find your daughter just yet. She's gone for a little walk. It won't take her long to get back – but she won't get back till my son is acquitted, and she won't get back at all if he's convicted."

The Judge said nothing. He was wondering what to do. Was the man telling the truth? Had he kidnapped Judy? What was the best course to take if he had?

"I'm quite desperate," went on Shepherd's father. "I will stop at nothing to get my son acquitted. Go to your lodging, if you like, and see if your daughter is still there. If she isn't, come and meet me again here. But come at once and don't bring anyone with you. I don't value my own life at all – or your daughter's. You have enough experience to know a determined man when you see one. And another word of warning. If you do manage to get me arrested you will never see her again. I've made sure of that. Now what about it? Shall we say in fifteen minutes' time?"

The Judge walked off without a word. He was terribly afraid, though hoping against hope that he would find Judy safe and sound. But she was not at his lodging nor did anyone know where she was.

"Ring up the police," he told his Marshal, "and say I may want to see the Chief Constable urgently. Don't say what it's about. I'm going out again."

You can imagine that, when the inquest on the little girl was held and the Judge's behaviour, when his daughter was found to be missing, was mentioned in evidence, it all tended to suggest that he had himself made away with her, particularly as he never did call in the police.

About a quarter of an hour after his first meeting with the man the Judge returned to the place where he had left him.

"Well?" said Shepherd's father. "Are you satisfied I mean business?" And then, as he sensed what was in the Judge's mind, he added, "Now, it's no use calling me names. You must just make up your mind whether you'll do a bargain with me or not. I've nothing to lose. If my son is hanged I shall kill myself, having first disposed of your daughter. I shan't enjoy doing that, but I assure you I shall do it, for, unless I can convince you that I will, there's no chance of your helping me."

Mr Justice Kingsdown was a most honourable man. The impartiality and incorruptibility of His Majesty's Judges is beyond question. Yet, now he was dealing with a madman whom he believed capable of murdering his daughter. Life would mean very little to him indeed without her. His wife had died in giving her birth, and the thought of losing Judy was beyond endurance. If he put the police on to it it might mean her death in any event. If Shepherd were convicted he was satisfied it would mean her death. What could he do? The Shepherd case was a bad one. The man's father was right in saying that it was unlikely that he would be acquitted. Even assuming he was prepared to break his judge's oath and try to help the man, even then, it was at least doubtful if any jury would let him off. Even supposing he summed up in such a manner as to make everyone who read the case think he had lost his senses, it was still possible that the jury would convict. Then he heard a voice very like his own – and it was his own, but it seemed to be someone else speaking – saying, "I am prepared to bargain with you."

"Good," said the man. "Your daughter will walk into your house alive and well within half an hour of my son's acquittal."

"It's not so simple as that," said the Judge. "I do not see how your son can be acquitted by the jury."

"What then?" said the man. "Can you influence the Home Secretary?"

"Not in the least," said the Judge, "nor would I try. But remember this. Every convicted man has the right of appeal to the Court of Criminal Appeal."

"I know that, but they'll make short work of his appeal."

The Judge hesitated. Then he heard himself saying, "That would no doubt be so, if the case turned out as it appears from the depositions and if I summed up properly. But you must know that, if I should sum up incorrectly in law, then the Court of Criminal Appeal would allow the appeal and, once allowed, your son would be free and there could be no fresh trial."

"Are you sure you can do it?"

"I can – and I shall have to. You will find that my summing up is strongly against the accused and you will not be able to recognise the mistakes I make in it. But I shall see to it that there are sufficient errors to enable the Appeal Court to allow the appeal."

"Very well. I will return your daughter within an hour of the appeal being allowed."

"Where is she now? Is she well? Are you ill-treating her?"

"Naturally, she's not very happy, but she is quite well and will not be ill-treated – provided you keep to your part of the bargain."

"Are you not afraid for yourself after it is all over?"

"Not in the least. First of all, I don't see how you can admit what you'll have done. Secondly, even if you did have the courage to do so, I shall have achieved my object and saved my son and I couldn't get more than imprisonment. So it's well worth it."

"If my daughter is not returned immediately your son is acquitted or his appeal allowed I will leave no stone unturned until you are brought to justice."

"You needn't worry. I'm a blackmailer all right, but not for money. And when I've got what I want – my son – I will leave you in peace."

"You had better," said the Judge, and returned to his lodging.

He spent a very troubled night. The whole thing seemed incredible – impossible – and yet he knew it was true. Judy was still missing, and he did not dare tell the police. Rightly or wrongly, he believed that the man would keep his word. He gave some explanation for Judy's absence and for his original message to the police. You can imagine how this looked at the inquests. Yes, I was very glad to put matters right, as far as his memory was concerned.

Next morning the trial began. Everything went very much as the public had expected. The Judge behaved quite normally, though he felt very far from normal. His pointed questions to the witnesses and later to the accused himself appeared to tell strongly against the latter. At the end of the evidence and counsel's speeches he began his summing up. Again everything seemed quite normal. When there is a strong case against a man the summing up of the Judge is bound to appear against him too. Halfway through his summing up, counsel for the prosecution appeared slightly surprised and whispered to his opponent. Almost immediately the Judge stopped and said, "If you wish to talk during my summing up I shall be obliged if you will do so outside." The whispering ceased, but later another look of surprise appeared on the face of prosecuting counsel. This time, however, he kept his feelings to himself – and on two more occasions too. The summing up was over. The jury retired. No one who had been in court had much doubt about the verdict. Half an hour later the jury pronounced Shepherd guilty. Mr Justice Kingsdown passed sentence of death, the court adjourned and he returned to his lodging, the words "And may the Lord have mercy on your soul" still ringing in his ears.

You may be wondering how I obtained all my information. Well, of course, the trial was public property and the original hearing of the inquest on the Judge and his daughter provided some of my material. The rest of it I obtained from Shepherd's father himself – whom I traced and arrested and had the pleasure of seeing sentenced to death. He made a full confession and I was quite satisfied as to its truth. If I had had any doubt about it, the newspaper on which the Judge's head was resting would have reassured me. The report of the hearing of Shepherd's appeal was given in full. It ended as follows: "Some criticism has been made by the Appellant's counsel of certain passages in the summing up of the learned Judge. It is quite true that the view of the law, as enunciated in these passages, is not to be found in the books. In the opinion of the Court, however, these passages, so far from vitiating the verdict, constitute a most useful pronouncement on the subject in question. They are in our view good sense and good law, and the Court is grateful to the learned Judge for providing new learning on a difficult subject. In the result, the appeal fails and will be dismissed."

CHAPTER SIXTEEN

The Presumption

"Humph!" said the Professor as he finished the story. "I should like to have read that judgment. I wonder what the point of law was. Oh, well, I shall never know."

He turned the light out but was still unable to sleep. After another hour or so he turned it on again. Then he made his decision. He would leave first thing next morning, spend one night here and one night there and at all costs refrain from telling stories. He decided to leave the Browns a note, as he seldom saw them for breakfast. He wrote apologising for his sudden departure and saying that he would write to them on his return to Cambridge. He didn't know the name of their house, but "Dr Brown, Soham," would be sufficient.

"Please don't comment on my sudden departure. I will explain it all to you when we meet again."

Then, as an afterthought, he added, "I'm so sorry I shan't be able to detain you for the next few nights, but here is one last story you can read to each other – and, don't forget, you mustn't go to bed until you've finished it."

He then wrote and attached to his letter "The Presumption."

The Presumption

This story concerns Captain Eric Parsons of the 2nd Loamshires, the Marquess of Salisbury, a Naval Officer, the Sultan of Zanzibar, and a rule of law which was made prominent in the Russell case. Their connection will not be immediately apparent, but if you persevere to the end you will see how it arose.

You probably remember the Russell case in 1924, when the House of Lords decided that neither a husband nor a wife could give evidence to show that any child born during wedlock was illegitimate. That case was also a good illustration of the rule that a child born to a married woman is presumed to be a lawful child of the marriage until the contrary is proved in court.

So much for the rule of law; now for some people.

Eric Parsons was a first-class regular officer. He had done excellently throughout the North African campaign and, when he was wounded just before the fall of Tunis, his CO wondered where he would find his equal as an Adjutant. At the same time he recommended him for a decoration. He had earned it. In July Eric went on a month's sick leave to Alexandria. There, at his hotel bar, he met a Wing Commander. Eric mentioned that he was spending the whole of his leave in Alexandria.

"Why?" said the Wing Commander.

"Well, it's the best place in Egypt."

"I dare say – but I'm going to England tomorrow, would you like to come? I'll bring you back before your month is up."

Eric thought quickly. He had already applied for such leave and it had been turned down. If he went and were found out it would be a very serious matter indeed. He would be court-martialled and his army career ruined – at the best. He had another drink. The temptation became greater. He could see his wife's look of amazed joy as he suddenly walked into the house. He had another drink. He thought of Alamein, Mareth and Akarit – he had been through them all – he thought of his wife – had another drink and he said, "Yes."

They went the next morning. The joy and amazement in his wife's face came well up to expectation. He had the happiest three weeks in his life. He had been anxious about his return, in case there should be a hitch, but there was none and in due course he returned to Alexandria and finished the last few days of his leave there. After a few weeks at the base depot he rejoined his battalion, which was then in Italy. He went right through that campaign without a scratch. Often he thought about those glorious three weeks.

One day in April he received a letter from his wife which made him think of them even more.

"I'm very sorry, darling," wrote his wife, "but I've had a baby – a boy. I didn't tell you before, as I know you'd have been worried, and you have quite enough to cope with. Now that it's all over successfully I realise that you may still be worried, as it will take some explaining. But I'm quite sure you'll be able to think of something. Don't forget to claim the extra allowance. I'm thrilled. Aren't you? Do you agree to Charles, Eric?"

The letter said a lot of other things, but they are not material to the story.

They were resting at the time when he received the letter and, although now a Major, he was acting as Adjutant in the temporary absence of his successor. He was certainly thrilled at having a son, but he felt a different sort of thrill when he visualised his CO's face on hearing of his trip to England. His first inclination was to say nothing about it and forgo the additional allowance. Then he realised that the baby's arrival must soon become known to his Colonel through the Colonel's wife. She kept in fairly close touch with his own wife. His failure to publish the necessary casualty would do no good and would merely deprive him of an additional and much needed allowance. But how could he explain everything to the Colonel? However much he liked him the CO would be bound to report the matter and he would be court-martialled. What on earth could he say when called upon for an explanation? It was while he was searching his brains for some answer to this apparently insoluble problem that he remembered the story of the Marquess of Salisbury, the Sultan of Zanzibar and the Naval Officer. You probably know it, for it is an old one, but, for the benefit of those who do not, here it is.

When the Marquess of Salisbury was Foreign Secretary, he had a little trouble with Zanzibar. Accordingly, one day he sent for a young Lieutenant-Commander who had command of a destroyer. Salisbury addressed him as follows: "Take your destroyer, go to Zanzibar, train your guns on the Sultan's palace and present him with this ultimatum. Good morning to you."

"Very good, sir," said the officer, and went towards the door. Then a thought struck him and he stopped and said – "Oh, sir, supposing the Sultan rejects the ultimatum?"

"Oh," said Salisbury, a little taken aback. "Oh – well – in that case you must turn round and come home again."

"Very good, sir," said the officer and went out. He duly took his destroyer to Zanzibar, trained his guns on the Sultan's palace and proceeded to seek an audience with the Sultan. On the audience being obtained, he informed the Sultan that the destroyer's guns were trained on the palace and handed him the ultimatum. The Sultan read it thoughtfully.

"And suppose," he asked, "I refuse to comply with the demands made in this document?"

"Then, sir," said the Lieutenant-Commander, looking extremely grave, "I should very regretfully have to put into force the second part of my instructions."

There was a pause; then the Sultan capitulated.

That Lieutenant-Commander was a man after Eric's own heart. He accordingly made the necessary official notification that his wife had had a baby and waited for the storm to break. He had not to wait long. The Colonel sent for him. It was obvious that he was extremely angry. He was probably quite as angry at the thought of losing Eric as at anything else.

"What," he almost shouted, "is the meaning of this?"

Eric looked troubled, but did not answer.

"Haven't you a tongue in your head? Will you kindly explain what this means before I report the matter any further?"

Eric continued to look extremely unhappy and, then, in a low voice which seemed almost to be breaking, he said: "I would very much rather that you didn't ask me anything about it, sir."

There was a pause. Suddenly the Colonel's wrath disappeared as quickly as it had come. He put his hand on Eric's shoulder.

"I'm sorry, old boy," he said. "I understand. Forget what I've said. Let's go and have a drink."

And they had several.

CHAPTER SEVENTEEN

Portrait In Silk

Immediately after breakfast the Professor saw Mr Bennett and paid his bill.

"I'm sorry I have to leave like this," he said, "but I shall certainly come again."

"I quite understand," said Mr Bennett. "I'm so sorry about last night's disturbance."

"Oh – not at all," said the Professor. " I was just a little tired. It was no bother really."

"Well, it's very nice of you to take it that way. Policemen are so very stupid, aren't they?"

"I've really had no experience of them," said the Professor.

"Well – this one was," said Mr Bennett.

"Indeed?" said the Professor.

"Very stupid," said Mr Bennett. "Quite incapable of putting two and two together. By the way – I don't think he mentioned to you the name of the lunatic, did he?"

"I don't think he did."

"But he had it, you know. He told me. It was Melton. Well – goodbye, Mr Mowbray, and do come again."

"Goodbye," said the Professor, "and thank you very much indeed."

"Not at all," said Mr Bennett. "I've been there myself."

"Good God!" said the Professor, and hurried off to catch his train. A very near thing – a very near thing indeed – he kept on saying to himself. However, a miss is as good as a mile, and four days later he called on his friends at Knightsbridge and told them his experiences.

"I shall go straight back to Cambridge," he said, "I feel sure I shall be all right."

"Don't you think you'd better try out a lecture on us first?" his friend asked. "You don't want to find the same thing happening."

"A very good idea," said the Professor. "If it won't bore you too much. Which would you prefer, jurisprudence or Roman law?"

"Oh, whichever you like."

"Very well, then, here goes," said the Professor. "An introduction to the principles of jurisprudence," and he began "Portrait in Silk."

Portrait In Silk

Sir George Woodward, KC, leaned comfortably back in his car as he was being driven home from the Law Courts and started to count his blessings. A dangerous thing to do. However, he was not superstitious and, being in a very happy frame of mind, he proceeded to analyse his happiness. A charming wife. That, of course, came first. Intelligent children. A very large practice at the Bar. An excellent reputation. Plenty of friends. Substantial means. A house in the country. A flat in town. Excellent health. Why hadn't he put that higher in the list? Loyal and well-trained servants – particularly the chauffeur who was then driving him. Not a very good driver, perhaps, but a sound mechanic and a willing worker, who took great pride in the new Daimler – which he was about to smash.

The collision occurred in Trafalgar Square. The Daimler was no match for the six-wheeled lorry which it had challenged. Sir George was removed unconscious to Charing Cross Hospital. He had quite an eventful period of unconsciousness. He found himself riding alone in a desert. Suddenly he was set upon by three horsemen, who appeared to be bandits.

"Will you come with us, Sir George?" said one of them.

"Is there any alternative?" he asked.

"There is – but it is rather painful."

"I will come."

"I am extremely obliged to you, Sir George," said the apparent leader of the three.

They rode for about an hour and arrived at a large building faintly reminiscent of the Law Courts. He did not have time to wonder why it should have been built in the heart of the desert or what purpose it served.

"Will you go into the robing-room, please, and get ready for the trial," he was told.

"Am I for the plaintiff or the defendant?"

"For the defendant. You will find your brief in the robing-room and your clerk is there too."

He walked into the building and, following the notices, he soon reached the robing-room. It also was faintly reminiscent of the one in the Law Courts. His clerk greeted him. "You're late, sir," he said.

"I'm sorry, but I was held up by bandits."

"I can't very well tell that to Mr Gumption," said the clerk. "I'd better make one of the usual excuses. Have you read the papers?"

"Of course not. I haven't had them yet."

"Well, you'll have to pretend you have. I've told Mr Gumption that you've been working on them."

"Very well. By the way, what is the brief marked?"

"I haven't arranged the fee yet."

"Is it a heavy case?"

"There's a lot of correspondence, but I don't think there's very much in it. I shall ask five hundred guineas, and accept three hundred if necessary. Now do take your tie off, please, sir – or you'll be late for the court."

"Where's the brief?"

"I've got it – I'll give it to you when you're robed." He put on his robes and the clerk handed him the brief.

"Rex *v* Woodward," it read.

"Why have you accepted this? You know I won't touch criminal work."

"Mr Gumption wanted you to do it as a special favour."

"I don't care two hoots about Mr Gumption. I won't do it."

"You'll have to now. Come along or you'll be late."

"But they don't try criminal cases here – unless it's an appeal. There must be some mistake."

"There's no mistake at all. Are you coming, sir, or not?"

"Oh, very well."

"Mr Gumption's waiting outside the court."

They went together out of the robing-room to the corridor outside the courts. They soon found Mr Gumption.

"Ah – good morning, Sir George," he said, as he shook hands. "It's nice of you to do this for us."

"Not at all, Mr Gumption, I'm only too pleased."

"I was rather afraid you wouldn't touch criminal work."

"Well, I don't ordinarily – but for your firm I don't mind making an exception."

"Very good of you, Sir George. What d'you think of the case?"

"Well, you know – I think it rather depends on how our man gives evidence."

"Exactly what I said," said Mr Gumption. "Will he make a good witness?"

"Only moderate, I think. He's a little too pleased with himself. Witnesses of that kind are always liable to make a mess of things."

"They are indeed. It's a pity I've not been able to talk to him before. However, we'll see what can be done." At that moment his clerk came up.

"Come along, sir," he said, "the Judge is waiting." They entered the court. The Judge was already sitting. Sir George was very surprised to find that he did not know him.

"Come along, Sir George," said the Judge. "I'm waiting."

"I'm extremely sorry, my Lord. There was a hold up on the line."

"That's all right, Sir George. I always used to think those last-minute chats outside the court were necessary when I was at the Bar. Now, let's get on. Mr Playfair, will you read out the charges?"

This is all very extraordinary, he thought. What is happening? Then he saw that the Judge was one of the bandits who had held him up.

"So you see who I am," said the Judge. "I look a bit different in a wig – don't I? Have you any objection to being tried by me?"

"To being tried by you, my Lord? I'm sure it's my fault, my Lord, but I don't understand what your Lordship means."

"It certainly is your fault, Sir George. If you would read your papers before coming into court it would save such a lot of time. Perhaps you will look at them now. It's never too late."

Sir George turned round to speak to his junior. He found that he was another of the bandits. "Would your Lordship excuse me if I consult my junior?"

"Certainly, Sir George. I'll adjourn for a few minutes if you like."

"No – thank you, my Lord, that will be quite unnecessary."

He turned to his junior.

What's this all about?" he asked.

"I don't know," came the reply. "I'm only a pupil. I'm afraid I've had nothing to do with the case. It's Mr Forsythe's."

"Where is Forsythe?"

"I don't know, I'm afraid. He's in two cases before the Official Referee, one in the Court of Appeal and there's a possibility of a jury case coming on as well."

Sir George turned to the Judge.

"Your Lordship must forgive me, but my junior appears to be too busy to attend the court."

"Ah – Mr Forsythe," said the Judge. "He is rather inclined to vanish. Never mind, Sir George, you can probably manage without him in this case. After all, it does concern you rather more than your junior. Just consult your brief again."

Sir George looked down at the papers.

"Rex v Woodward."

His own name. But that was absurd. He couldn't appear for himself – and anyway he hadn't done anything wrong. Then he looked at the place where the fee should have been written. What he saw was "Fee. Nothing if you lose. Life if you win. Consultation two guineas."

"You see, Sir George, you're being tried for your life,"

said the Judge. "If you are convicted there is only one sentence possible. Death. Most unpleasant, but there it is. We all feel for you. Would you like to sit down?"

"No doubt I'm being extremely dense," said Sir George, "but I haven't the faintest idea what your Lordship is talking about."

"Well, I'll make you understand," said the Judge sharply, and his face suddenly took on a fiendish look.

"You are being tried for your life. If you are unable to give a good account of yourself you will be hanged. Is that clear so far?"

"I suppose so, my Lord, but it's very bewildering."

"Well, it will be made clearer if and when necessary. Should you succeed in satisfying the court as to your past conduct you will go free. Now do you understand?"

"I am to justify my existence, my Lord?"

"Precisely," said the Judge, "if you can."

"I think I can do that, my Lord, unless the court takes the view that no barrister can do it."

"I don't think I can go as far as to say that," said the Judge. "Lawyers are as necessary as lavatory attendants. Their work in some respects is much the same. No – you may take it that it is your own personal career which you must justify."

"Very good, my Lord. I have been at the Bar for twenty-eight years, and during that time it has never been suggested from the Bench or from the Bar that I have not conducted my practice honourably and fairly. Such measure of success as I have attained has been attained by scrupulous methods and hard work. I have a reasonably quick mind and a brain which happens to be suited to the technique of the law. I have conducted some of the most important cases during the last fifteen years and have been briefed by most of the leading solicitors in the country. My private life is unassailable. I am as selfish as most men, but no more. I have paid proper regard to the education of my family. I – "

"Sir George, I need not trouble you about your private life at the moment. I would like to ask you a few questions about your career."

"Certainly, my Lord."

"I take it, Sir George, that you have never persuaded one of your own witnesses to commit perjury in order to assist your client's case."

"Certainly not, my Lord."

"On the other hand, have you never persuaded a witness to give rather different evidence from that which he originally proposed to give? I don't mean to tell a radically different story, but to make slight alterations in his proposed evidence."

"Well, my Lord, I have no doubt that, in questioning a client in my chambers before a case came on, I have brought out other facts or shed a different light on the same facts. In consequence, the witness' evidence has not been exactly the same as the evidence he would have given without such assistance."

"Can you say that you have always been satisfied that the story, as amended by you, has been a true one?"

"No, my Lord – any more than I could be conclusively satisfied as to the truth of the original story."

"Let me pass to another matter then, Sir George. Have you ever deliberately taken a false point on behalf of your client?"

"Every barrister does at times."

"Then the answer is 'yes,' Sir George. Do you seek to justify such conduct?"

"Yes, my Lord. If I were to refuse to take points on my client's behalf because I thought them false, I should be trying the case instead of the Judge. My view that a point is a bad one may be wrong. My client has a right that every conceivable point be taken on his behalf and the Judge will then decide which of them, if any, are sound points."

"Another question, Sir George. Have you ever interrupted opposing counsel – not because such interruption was really called for but in order to put him off?"

"My Lord, that is one of the less reputable tricks of advocacy in which I must confess I have occasionally indulged."

"Your object there must have been to win your case and not simply to obtain a just decision."

"I must admit that it has always been my object to win the case for my client, even though I considered he was in the wrong. I submit, however, my Lord, that with the present system of advocacy this is inevitable. I also say that I have rarely indulged in the tricks to which you have referred or in other similar tricks."

"Very well, then. Have you ever taken advantage of a misunderstanding by a witness which was not realised by the Judge?"

"I expect so, my Lord, on a few occasions. I give the same excuse. My view that the witness misunderstood may have been wrong."

"Have you then investigated the matter on such occasions so that it might be clearly shown whether your view was right or wrong? Or have you simply seized the advantage and hoped that your opponent would not be able to wrest it from you?"

"In my earlier days I may sometimes have adopted the latter course. I admit that it was wrong."

"Very well, Sir George. Taking your answers as a whole, I am inclined to form a lenient view of your actual conduct of cases. It seems to have been no worse than anyone else's and considerably better than many. Possibly that is due to the measure of success which you have achieved, but, whatever the cause, I am not disposed to decide against you so far. Now let me come to another matter. Have you ever accepted considerable sums which you have not earned? In other words, have you accepted briefs and the fees for such briefs and have you then failed to put in an appearance at the court for a considerable portion of the case

"I must plead guilty to that, my Lord."

"Your failure to attend was presumably due to your appearing in some other case or cases for which you were also paid."

"Yes, my Lord."

"Not very satisfactory conduct, is it, Sir George?"

"No, my Lord, but extremely difficult to avoid on some occasions. Moreover, many clients would prefer me to appear for two days out of a four-day case than to say I could not appear at all. Besides, if I refused cases because they might clash with others, I could never accept more than one brief at a time."

"I see no objection to that, Sir George."

"But, my Lord, it would mean that possibly during the whole of one month I would be doing nothing at all. To be absolutely certain that cases would not clash I could never accept a case which was set down for trial until I had no other case in that state of readiness. I can assure you, my Lord, that if I so acted many litigants would unnecessarily be deprived of my services."

"Then do you say, Sir George, that on the occasions to which we have been referring your failure to appear has been more or less an accident or, if not an accident, has had the full approval of your client?"

"In most cases, my Lord, yes."

"But not always?"

"I cannot truthfully say always, my Lord."

"Can you justify your conduct in the exceptional cases then?"

"I cannot, my Lord. I can only say that I am no worse an offender than anyone else and far less of an offender than some counsel whom I know – particularly those with political aspirations."

"I am not interested in others, Sir George – only in you. I must tell you quite plainly that I do not like rich men who take money for work they have not done. It would be unfortunate, would it not, if a surgeon left an operation for appendicitis in the middle in order to earn a fee for dealing with a mastoid. In such circumstances the death of the patient might result. The parallel in your work is the case being lost. I don't like it at all, Sir George. Now another matter. You have a very extensive and lucrative practice, have you not?"

"Yes, my Lord."

"Worth many thousand pounds a year?"

"Yes, my Lord."

"And you have earned this large income for a good many years?"

"Yes, my Lord."

"On how many occasions have you offered your services to the Poor Persons Department?"

"I cannot say exactly, my Lord, but not very often."

"Did you at any time in your career place your name upon the list of counsel ready to do work for nothing in Poor Persons cases?"

"No, my Lord."

"Why not?"

"My Lord, except in the Divorce and Criminal Courts,

barristers who acquire large practices very rarely do place their names upon this list. It is usually filled by the younger or less successful members of the profession. Barristers in my position usually do cases for no fee because we take a special interest in them, either of our own initiative or because we have been asked to do so by a friend."

"How many cases during the past ten years have you done for nothing?"

"I cannot say exactly, my Lord."

"Have you averaged as many as three a year?"

"I could not be sure, my Lord."

"What possible excuse have you for not giving more of your assistance? You have been a wealthy man for years. You could have undertaken many cases for no reward, with the only result that you would not have been quite so rich."

"I'm afraid that is the case, my Lord."

"You do not seem at all perturbed about it, Sir George, but I can assure you that you will have cause to be if you have no good excuse to offer."

"There is nothing else I can say, my Lord. I admit that I ought to have done more. It has simply not been customary in the profession."

"Well, it is high time that it was, Sir George, and perhaps, if I make an example of you, it will become customary. Have you anything to say why sentence should not be passed on you according to law?"

"Nothing more, my Lord."

"Very well, then. I could forgive a great deal in your behaviour in view of the existing system of law, but I cannot and will not forgive your disgraceful meanness. You will be hanged, Sir George. And at once. Would you like your wig on for the ceremony or not?"

"My Lord, is it possible to ask for another chance? I have been frank with the court. I realise my offence and will endeavour to amend my ways in the future."

"You should have thought of that before, Sir George. You will find the gallows in the main hall. If you would like a wash first, there is no objection."

"May I have permission to see my wife, my Lord?"

"Certainly. She is waiting to say goodbye to you at the gallows. I thought you would prefer your children not to witness the ceremony. Is there anything else I can do for you? You can have a copy of my judgment on the usual terms of 9d a folio. But I'm afraid your appeal, if any, will only be of academic interest, as you will be dead when it comes on for hearing."

"There is nothing else, my Lord."

"Very well, then, proceed to the place of execution, please."

In a daze Sir George walked to the entrance hall. The sight of his wife almost made him faint, but he managed to control himself sufficiently to arrive at the gallows unassisted. The noose was slipped round his neck, and, as the cold sweat gathered on his forehead and he looked for a last agonising time at his wife, he slowly regained consciousness and awoke to find her bending over him in Charing Cross Hospital.

He soon recovered. It was nothing worse than slight concussion. Three weeks later he was back at work again completely well – though he never forgot his appalling nightmare. A few days after he had returned to the Temple, his clerk came to him and said, "Stephen and Pettigrew have asked whether you would do a Poor Persons case for them. I said I was afraid you were too busy."

"Quite right," said Sir George, and turned his mind again to the case on which he was working.

CHAPTER EIGHTEEN

"Oh, dear," said the Professor. "I've done it again." "I'm not so sure," said his friend. "You're getting much nearer to the subject. That was far more like a dialogue on the morality of a barrister's practice than a short story. I believe that, if you persevere for a few days, you'll be cured. That's only a guess, mind you, but I think I'm probably right."

"I hope you are," said the Professor. "I think, you know, if I get back to Cambridge and spend a few days quietly in the right atmosphere it will come back to me. If I explain things to them I'm sure they won't have me recertified."

"There's a risk," said his friend.

"I shall take it," said the Professor. "In any event, I don't think I'm certifiable – just because I can't lecture on jurisprudence. If that were a fair test a lot of people would have been certified before now. Yes – I shall go straight back tomorrow morning. I can't tell you how grateful I am to you both. You've no idea what it was like in Tapworth House."

Next morning he set off in fairly high spirits. He was looking forward to his return. His holiday at "The Bear" had been pleasant, but all the time there had been hanging over him the shadow of Tapworth House. Now he was a free man again. As the train drew into Cambridge station he stepped on to the platform. No doubt his eagerness to return was the cause of his stepping off the train before it had come to a standstill. He was thrown quite heavily to the ground and his head struck something hard. He was dazed for the moment but not rendered unconscious. Porters soon arrived to give assistance and he was lifted up and taken into the waiting-room. There, to his relief, he found that he had merely bruised his body and bumped his head. There were no bones broken and the bump on his head, though unpleasant, was no more than a bump. He had a curious feeling of having been through exactly the same experience before. This feeling persisted right up till the time he had arrived at St James' and interviewed the Master.

Now, whether he had, in fact, been through the same experience before or whether all that has appeared in the foregoing pages went on only in the half-conscious brain of Professor Melton when he fell to the ground for the first and only time, must, I am afraid, remain a matter for speculation. True it is, however, that no attempt was made to certify or (if you take the other view) recertify the Professor. His lectures on jurisprudence and Roman law evoked the highest praise from the Law Faculty and bored the bulk of his audience to tears. In which happy pursuit we must regretfully, or (if you take the other view) cheerfully, leave him.

Henry Cecil

According to the Evidence

Alec Morland is on trial for murder. He has tried to remedy the ineffectiveness of the law by taking matters into his own hands. Unfortunately for him, his alleged crime was not committed in immediate defence of others or of himself. In this fascinating murder trial you will not find out until the very end just how the law will interpret his actions. Will his defence be accepted or does a different fate await him?

The Asking Price

Ronald Holbrook is a fifty-seven-year-old bachelor who has lived in the same house for twenty years. Jane Doughty, the daughter of his next-door neighbours, is seventeen. She suddenly decides she is in love with Ronald and wants to marry him. Everyone is amused at first but then events take a disturbingly sinister turn and Ronald finds himself enmeshed in a potentially tragic situation.

> 'The secret of Mr Cecil's success lies in continuing to do superbly what everyone now knows he can do well.'
> – *The Sunday Times*

Henry Cecil

Brief Tales from the Bench

What does it feel like to be a Judge? Read these stories and you can almost feel you are looking at proceedings from the lofty position of the Bench.

With a collection of eccentric and amusing characters, Henry Cecil brings to life the trials in a County Court and exposes the complex and often contradictory workings of the English legal system.

'Immensely readable. His stories rely above all on one quality – an extraordinary, an arresting, a really staggering ingenuity.'
– *New Statesman*

Brothers in Law

Roger Thursby, aged twenty-four, is called to the bar. He is young, inexperienced and his love life is complicated. He blunders his way through a succession of comic adventures including his calamitous debut at the bar.

His career takes an upward turn when he is chosen to defend the caddish Alfred Green at the Old Bailey. In this first Roger Thursby novel Henry Cecil satirizes the legal profession with his usual wit and insight.

'Uproariously funny.' – *The Times*

'Full of charm and humour. I think it is the best Henry Cecil yet.' – P G Wodehouse

Henry Cecil

Hunt the Slipper

Harriet and Graham have been happily married for twenty years. One day Graham fails to return home and Harriet begins to realise she has been abandoned. This feeling is strengthened when she starts to receive monthly payments from an untraceable source. After five years on her own Harriet begins to see another man and divorces Graham on the grounds of his desertion. Then one evening Harriet returns home to find Graham sitting in a chair, casually reading a book. Her initial relief turns to anger and then to fear when she realises that if Graham's story is true, she may never trust his sanity again. This complex comedy thriller will grip your attention to the very last page.

Sober as a Judge

Roger Thursby, the hero of *Brothers in Law* and *Friends at Court*, continues his career as a High Court judge. He presides over a series of unusual cases, including a professional debtor and an action about a consignment of oranges which turned to juice before delivery. There is a delightful succession of eccentric witnesses as the reader views proceedings from the Bench.

'The author's gift for brilliant characterisation makes this a book that will delight lawyers and laymen as much as did its predecessors.' – *The Daily Telegraph*

3363515R00129

Printed in Great Britain
by Amazon.co.uk, Ltd.,
Marston Gate.